MDA Explained

The Addison-Wesley Object Technology Series

Grady Booch, Ivar Jacobson, and James Rumbaugh, Series Editors

For more information, check out the series Web site [http://www.awprofessional.com/otseries/].

The Component Software Series

Clemens Szyperski, Series Editor

For more information, check out the series Web site [http://www.awprofessional.com/csseries/].

MDA Explained

The Model Driven Architecture™: Practice and Promise

Anneke Kleppe
Jos Warmer
Wim Bast

✦Addison-Wesley

Boston • San Francisco • New York • Toronto • Montreal
London • Munich • Paris • Madrid
Capetown • Sydney • Tokyo • Singapore • Mexico City

Many of the designations used by manufacturers and sellers to distinguish their products are claimed as trademarks. Where those designations appear in this book, and Addison-Wesley was aware of a trademark claim, the designations have been printed with initial capital letters or in all capitals.

MDA™, UML™, and MOF™ are either registered trademarks or trademarks of Object Management Group, Inc. in the United States and/or other countries.

The authors and publisher have taken care in the preparation of this book, but make no expressed or implied warranty of any kind and assume no responsibility for errors or omissions. No liability is assumed for incidental or consequential damages in connection with or arising out of the use of the information or programs contained herein.

The publisher offers discounts on this book when ordered in quantity for bulk purchases and special sales. For more information, please contact:

> U.S. Corporate and Government Sales
> (800) 382-3419
> corpsales@pearsontechgroup.com

For sales outside of the U.S., please contact:

> International Sales
> (317) 581-3793
> international@pearsontechgroup.com

Visit Addison-Wesley on the Web: www.awprofessional.com

Library of Congress Cataloging-in-Publication Data
Kleppe, Anneke G.
    MDA explained: the model driven architecture: practice and promise
Jos Warmer, Wim Bast
    p. cm.
    Includes bibliographical references and index.
    ISBN0-321-19442-X (alk. paper)
    1. Computer software--Development. 2. Computer architecture. I. Warmer, Jos B. II. Bast, Wim III Title
QA76.76.D47K5635 2003
005.1--dc21   2003043725

Copyright © 2003 by Pearson Education, Inc.

For information on obtaining permission for use of material from this work, please submit a written request to:

> Pearson Education, Inc.
> Rights and Contracts Department
> 75 Arlington Street, Suite 300
> Boston, MA 02116
> Fax: (617) 848-7047

ISBN 0-321-19442-X
Text printed on recycled paper
1 2 3 4 5 6 7 8 9 10—CRS—0706050403
First printing, April 2003

Contents

Chapter 2
The MDA Framework 15

Chapter 3
MDA Today 33

Foreword

"The sooner you start, the longer it takes." This paradoxical slogan was coined by Fred Brooks in 1975 in his seminal software engineering text, *The Mythical Man Month*, to emphasize that in software projects preparation is never wasted. If you skimp on requirements capture, you'll waste effort designing things the customer doesn't want. If you skimp on design, you'll write a lot of pointless code that doesn't solve his problem . . . and so on.

Dr. Brooks' dictum reminds us that Good Design Matters. It's just as true now as it was twenty-five years ago, but much else has changed. His book was based on his experience with OS/360, at that time one of the largest software projects ever undertaken. Since then, software size and complexity have grown beyond recognition, as has the bewildering choice of implementation technologies. Should we be using C++, Java, Visual Basic, or C#? CORBA? .NET? Web services? ebXML? EJB? JavaScript? ASP? JSP? SQL? ODBC? JDBC? Today, a single software project typically uses several of these, placing each where its particular strengths are best used. We have also become increasingly aware of the importance of software maintenance. Mission-critical software can continue in use for decades, suffering constant upgrades to cope with shifting requirements and changing technologies, so that in time maintenance costs exceed all others combined.

This book describes the Model Driven Architecture (MDA) approach to creating good designs that cope with multiple-implementation technologies and extended software lifetimes. MDA is based on widely-used industry standards for visualizing, storing, and exchanging software designs and models. The best-known of these standards is the Unified Modeling Language (UML). The Object Management Group's (OMG) creation of UML has promoted good design by providing a common, widely-understood visual language for engineers to exchange and document their ideas, and this has led to a dramatic increase in the use of visual modeling. However, visual modeling has too often been seen merely as a way to draw pictures of software, pictures that must later be laboriously translated into runnable code. One of the traditional excuses for skimping on design is that comprehensive models are "just paper," and effort spent creating them could better be spent on writing real code. Partly as a result of this, there's a trend today towards development techniques that emphasize creating executable code instead of "mere" designs.

In contrast, MDA heavily emphasizes creating designs—not paper designs, but machine-readable models stored in standardized repositories. The intellectual effort invested in these models doesn't just sit passively on the page waiting to be laboriously recast as code. Instead, MDA models are understood by automatic tools from multiple vendors that generate schemas, code skeletons, test harnesses, integration code, and deployment scripts for the multiple platforms used in a typical project. Design effort invested in MDA models is repeatedly reused to generate multiple components, and by being updated over the life of an application, provides accurate documentation of how much-maintained software really works, rather than a frozen image of how things looked at the end of the design phase. In short, MDA is an architecture for creating good designs in today's multiplatform IT environment.

The authors of this book are well qualified to describe and document the MDA vision. They have contributed to OMG's creation of MDA, worked on commercial products that implement it, and used it in practice. The book is founded on solid theory, but it is nevertheless a practitioners' handbook, built around real-world examples, and offering guidance to IT professionals facing the ever-present problems of bringing in next year's project on time and on budget. Time spent reading it will not be time wasted. Remember: the sooner you start, the longer it takes.

Andrew Watson
OMG Vice President & Technical Director
35,000 ft. over Greenland
November 17th, 2002

Preface

For many years, the three of us have been developing software using object-oriented techniques. We started with object-oriented programming languages like C++, Small-talk, and Eiffel. Soon we felt the need to describe our software at a higher level of abstraction. Even before the first object-oriented analysis and design methods like Coad/Yourdon and Object Modeling Technique (OMT) were published, we used our own invented bubble and arrow diagrams. This naturally led to questions like, "What does this arrow mean?" and "What is the difference between this circle and that rect-angle?" We therefore rapidly decided to use the newly emerging methods to design and describe our software.

Over the years we found that we were spending more time on designing our models than on writing code. The models helped us to cope with larger and more complex systems. Having a good model of the software available made the process of writing code easier, and in many cases, even straightforward.

In 1997 some of us got involved in defining the first standard for object-oriented modeling called Unified Modeling Language (UML). This was a major milestone that stimulated the use of modeling in the software industry. When the OMG launched its initiative on Model Driven Architecture (MDA), we felt that this was logically the next step to take. People try to get more and more value from their high-level models, and the MDA approach supports these efforts.

At that moment we realized that all these years we had been naturally walking the path toward model-driven development. Every bit of wisdom we acquired during our struggle with the systems we had to build fitted in with this new idea of how to build software. It caused a feeling similar to an AHA-experience: "Yes, this is it!"—the same feeling we had years before when we first encountered the object-oriented way of thinking, and again when we first read the GOF book on design patterns. We feel that MDA could very well be the next major step forward in the way software is being developed. MDA brings the focus of software development to a higher level of abstraction, thereby raising the level of maturity of the IT industry.

We are aware of the fact that the grand vision of MDA, which Richard Soley, the president of the OMG, presents so eloquently, is not yet a reality. However, some parts of MDA can already be used today, while others are under development. With this book we want to give you insight into what MDA means and what you can achieve, both today and in the future.

Anneke Kleppe
Jos Warmer
Wim Bast
Soest, the Netherlands, March 2003

Introduction

Model Driven Architecture (MDA) is a fairly new asset in the field of computer science. This book explains the fundamentals of MDA in a broad perspective. Answers to questions like "What are models and how do they relate to code?" are given. The advantages of MDA and how these advantages can be realized, are discussed.

The concept of transformation of models is central to the realization of the benefits of MDA. We will explain what a transformation is, which types of transformations exist, and the way in which transformations can be defined. Yet the book remains critical towards the types and forms of transformations that will and will not lead to substantial benefits for the industry. Finally, the book contains a number of examples of transformations that are interesting in themselves.

WHO SHOULD READ THIS BOOK

The book is meant to be read by a wide audience. It is meant for anyone who wants to know what MDA is about and who wants to know the role of the different Object Management Group (OMG) standards and the tools that claim to support them. Technical managers will get an understanding of MDA that helps them judge when and how it can best be applied in their projects. It is also a book for the more experienced software developer who is interested in modeling and programming on a higher level of abstraction. Knowledge of the Unified Modeling Language (UML) and the Object Constraint Language (OCL) is presumed. Knowledge of Java, Enterprise Java Beans (EJB), SQL, and Java Server Pages (JSP) is helpful, especially for the examples, but not necessary.

HOW THIS BOOK SHOULD BE USED

Surely a book like this is meant to be read, and to be interesting, from the start to the end, so we would like to encourage you to read it as a whole. However, we realize that not everyone has either the time or the technical background to read everything. Therefore, we would like to suggest three major tracks:

- Managers track: Managers who do not want to go into all details of the technology behind MDA should read Chapter 1 through Chapter 3, Chapter 11, and Chapter 12. Optionally, they might want to read Chapter 4.
- Developers track: People who are more interested in the application of MDA for developing software will want to read Chapter 1 through Chapter 7, Chapter 11, and Chapter 12.
- Specialists track: To get a thorough understanding of the technical background of MDA, you should read the entire book.

The details of the examples in Chapter 5, Chapter 6, and Chapter 10 can be skimmed through. This will not hinder understanding of the remainder of the book. However, it is important to realize that in real-life applications of MDA all of the details of these example chapters do exist, although they might sometimes be encapsulated into a black box.

TYPEFACE CONVENTIONS

This book uses the following typeface conventions:

- All code examples are printed in a `monospaced font`.
- At the first introduction or definition of a term, the term is shown in *italics*.
- All references to classes, attributes, and other elements of a model are shown in *italics*.
- General emphasis is shown in *italics*.

No other typeface conventions are being used.

INFORMATION ON RELATED SUBJECTS

More information on MDA can be found in books mentioned in the bibliography and on the following Web site from the OMG:

- http://www.omg.org/mda

BOOK SUPPORT AND EXAMPLE IMPLEMENTATION

The Rosa's Breakfast example from Chapter 4 through Chapter 6 and Chapter 10 can be executed using the OptimalJ tool. A free trial version of the tool, including the complete example, can be downloaded from the following Web page:

- http://www.klasse.nl/mdaexplained

ACKNOWLEDGMENTS

We would like to thank our reviewers for the time they have spent reading different versions of this book. Without their constructive feedback, this book would not be what it is today. We have benefited greatly from the insights that they shared with us. We would like to thank Frank Baerveld, Jeroen Bruijning, Aldo Eisma, Ghica van Emde-Boas, Peter van Emde-Boas, Martin Gogolla, Martin Matula, Hans van Oosten, and Andrew Watson. Special thanks goes to Heinrich Hußmann who made the effort of reading the first draft even though much of his attention was directed to trying to keep his feet and equipment dry during the flooding of Dresden in the summer of 2002. Another person that deserves our special thanks is John Daniels, whose thorough and positive criticism has led us to rewrite large parts of the first draft of the book.

We also want to thank the team from Addison-Wesley for their help, especially Mary O'Brien, who became our editor at a very late stage, but arranged every detail of our collaboration smoothly.

The MDA Development Process

This chapter describes some of the major problems in software development. It explains the concepts of the Model Driven Architecture (MDA), and discusses how MDA can help to solve these problems.

1.1 Traditional Software Development

Software development is often compared with hardware development in terms of maturity. While in hardware development there has been much progress, e.g., processor speed has grown exponentially in twenty years, the progress made in software development seems to be minimal. To some extent this is a matter of appearances. The progress made in software development cannot be measured in terms of development speed or costs.

Progress in software development is evident from the fact that it is feasible to build much more complex and larger systems. Just think how quickly and efficiently we would be able to build a monolithic mainframe application that has no graphical user interface and no connections to other systems. We never do this anymore, and that is why we do not have solid figures to support the idea that progress has been made.

Still, software development is an area in which we are struggling with a number of major problems. Writing software is labor intensive. With each new technology, much work needs to be done again and again. Systems are never built using only one technology and systems always need to communicate with other systems. There is also the problem of continuously changing requirements.

To show how MDA addresses these problems, we will analyze some of the most important problems with software development and discover the cause of these problems.

1.1.1 The Productivity Problem

The software development process as we know it today is often driven by low-level design and coding. A typical process, as illustrated in Figure 1-1, includes a number of phases:

1. Conceptualization and requirements gathering
2. Analysis and functional description
3. Design
4. Coding
5. Testing
6. Deployment

Whether we use an incremental and iterative version of this process, or the traditional waterfall process, documents and diagrams are produced during phases 1 through 3. These include requirements descriptions in text and pictures, and often many Unified Modeling Language (UML) diagrams like use cases, class diagrams, interaction diagrams, activity diagrams, and so on. The stack of paper produced is sometimes impressive. However, most of the artifacts from these phases is *just paper* and nothing more.

The documents and corresponding diagrams created in the first three phases rapidly lose their value as soon as the coding starts. The connection between the diagrams and the code fades away as the coding phase progresses. Instead of being an exact specification of the code, the diagrams usually become more or less unrelated pictures.

When a system is changed over time, the distance between the code and the text and diagrams produced in the first three phases becomes larger. Changes are often done at the code level only, because the time to update the diagrams and other high-level documents is not available. Also, the added value of updated diagrams and documents is questionable, because any new change starts in the code anyway. So why do we use so much precious time building high-level specifications?

The idea of Extreme Programming (XP) (Beck 2000) has become popular in a rapid fashion. One of the reasons for this is that it acknowledges the fact that the code is the driving force of software development. The only phases in the development process that are really productive are coding and testing.

As Alistair Cockburn states in *Agile Software Development* (Cockburn 2002), the XP approach solves only part of the problem. As long as the same team works on the software, there is enough high-level knowledge in their heads to understand the system. During initial development this is often the case. The problems start when the team is dismantled, which usually happens after delivery of the first release of the software. Other people need to maintain (fix bugs, enhance functionality, and so on) the

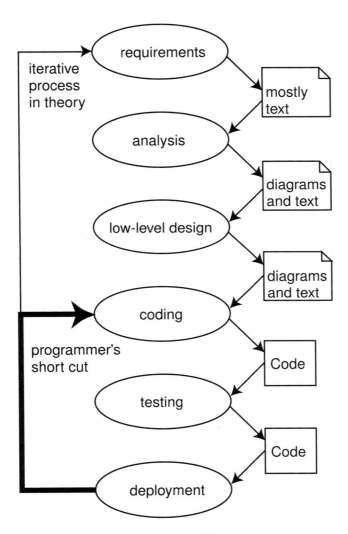

Figure 1-1 *Traditional software development life cycle*

software. Having just code and tests makes maintenance of a software system very difficult. Given five-hundred thousand lines of code (or even much more), where do you start to try and understand how a system works?

Alistair Cockburn talks about "markers" that need to be left behind for new people who will work on the software. These markers often take the form of text and higher-level diagrams. Without them you are literally lost. It is like being dropped in a foreign city without a map or road signs that show the directions.

So, either we use our time in the first phases of software development building high-level documentation and diagrams, or we use our time in the maintenance phase finding out what the software is actually doing. Neither way we are directly productive in the sense that we are producing code. Developers often consider these tasks as being overhead. Writing code is being productive, writing models or documentation is not. Still, in a mature software project these tasks need to be done.

1.1.2 The Portability Problem

The software industry has a special characteristic that makes it stand apart from most other industries. Each year, and sometimes even faster, new technologies are being invented and becoming popular (for example Java, Linux, XML, HTML, SOAP, UML, J2EE, .NET, JSP, ASP, Flash, Web Services, and so on). Many companies need to follow these new technologies for good reasons:

- The technology is demanded by the customers (e.g., Web interfaces).
- It solves some real problems (e.g., XML for interchange or Java for portability).
- Tool vendors stop supporting old technologies and focus on the new one (e.g., UML support replaces OMT).

The new technologies offer tangible benefits for companies and many of them cannot afford to lag behind. Therefore, people have to jump on these new technologies quite fast. As a consequence, the investments in previous technologies lose value and they may even become worthless.

The situation is even more complex because the technologies themselves change as well. They come in different versions, without a guarantee that they are backwards compatible. Tool vendors usually only support the two or three most recent versions.

As a consequence, existing software is either ported to the new technology, or to a newer version of an existing technology. The software may remain unchanged utilizing the older technology, in which case the existing, now legacy, software needs to interoperate with new systems that will be built using new technology.

1.1.3 The Interoperability Problem

Software systems rarely live in isolation. Most systems need to communicate with other, often already existing, systems. As a typical example we have seen that over the past years many companies have been building new Web-based systems. The new end-user application runs in a Web browser (using various technologies like HTML, ASP, JSP, and so on) and it needs to get its information from existing back-end systems.

Even when systems are completely built from scratch, they often span multiple technologies, sometimes both old and new. For example, when a system uses Enterprise Java Beans (EJB), it also needs to use relational databases as a storage mechanism.

Over the years we have learned not to build huge monolithic systems. Instead we try to build components that do the same job by interacting with each other. This makes it easier (or at all possible) to make changes to a system. The different components are all built using the best technology for the job, but need to interact with each other. This has created a need for interoperability.

1.1.4 The Maintenance and Documentation Problem

In the previous sections, we touched upon the problem of maintenance. Documentation has always been a weak link in the software development process. It is often done as an afterthought. Most developers feel their main task is to produce code. Writing documentation during development costs time and slows down the process. It does not support the developer's main task. The availability of documentation supports the task of those that come later. So, writing documentation feels like doing something for the sake of prosperity, not for your own sake. There is no incentive to writing documentation other than your manager, who tells you that you must.

This is one of the main reasons why documentation is often not of very good quality. The only persons that can check the quality are fellow developers who hate the job of writing documentation just as much. This also is the reason that documentation is often not kept up to date. With every change in the code the documentation needs to be changed as well—by hand!

The developers are wrong, of course. Their task is to develop systems that can be changed and maintained afterwards. Despite the feelings of many developers, writing documentation is one of their essential tasks.

A solution to this problem at the code level is the facility to generate the documentation directly from the source code, ensuring that it is always up to date. The documentation is in effect part of the code and not a separate entity. This is supported in several programming languages, like Eiffel and Java. This solution, however, only solves the low-level documentation problem. The higher-level documentation (text and diagrams) still needs to be maintained by hand. Given the complexity of the systems that are built, documentation at a higher level of abstraction is an absolute must.

1.2 THE MODEL DRIVEN ARCHITECTURE

The Model Driven Architecture (MDA) is a framework for software development defined by the Object Management Group (OMG). Key to MDA is the importance of models in the software development process. Within MDA the software development process is driven by the activity of modeling your software system.

In this section we first explain the basic MDA development life cycle, and next illustrate how MDA can help to solve (at least part of) the problems mentioned in the previous sections.

1.2.1 The MDA Development Life Cycle

The MDA development life cycle, which is shown in Figure 1-2, does not look very different from the traditional life cycle. The same phases are identified. One of the major differences lies in the nature of the artifacts that are created during the development process. The artifacts are formal models, i.e., models that can be understood by computers. The following three models are at the core of the MDA.

Platform Independent Model

The first model that MDA defines is a model with a high level of abstraction that is independent of any implementation technology. This is called a Platform Independent Model (PIM).

A PIM describes a software system that supports some business. Within a PIM, the system is modeled from the viewpoint of how it best supports the business. Whether a system will be implemented on a mainframe with a relational database or on an EJB application server plays no role in a PIM.

Platform Specific Model

In the next step, the PIM is transformed into one or more Platform Specific Models (PSMs). A PSM is tailored to specify your system in terms of the implementation constructs that are available in one specific implementation technology. For example, an EJB PSM is a model of the system in terms of EJB structures. It typically contains EJB-specific terms like "home interface," "entity bean," "session bean," and so on. A relational database PSM includes terms like "table," "column," "foreign key," and so on. It is clear that a PSM will only make sense to a developer who has knowledge about the specific platform.

A PIM is transformed into one or more PSMs. For each specific technology platform a separate PSM is generated. Most of the systems today span several technologies, therefore it is common to have many PSMs with one PIM.

Code

The final step in the development is the transformation of each PSM to code. Because a PSM fits its technology rather closely, this transformation is relatively straightforward.

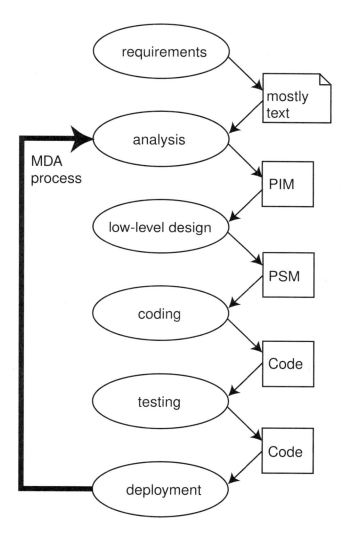

Figure 1-2 *MDA software development life cycle*

The MDA defines the PIM, PSM, and code, and also defines how these relate to each other. A PIM should be created, then transformed into one or more PSMs, which then are transformed into code. The most complex step in the MDA development process is the one in which a PIM is transformed into one or more PSMs.

Raising the Level of Abstraction

The PIM, PSM, and code are shown as artifacts of different steps in the development life cycle. More importantly, they represent different abstraction levels in the system specification. The ability to transform a high level PIM into a PSM raises the level of abstraction at which a developer can work. This allows a developer to cope with more complex systems with less effort.

1.2.2 Automation of the Transformation Steps

The MDA process may look suspiciously much like traditional development. However, there is a crucial difference. Traditionally, the transformations from model to model, or from model to code, are done mainly by hand. Many tools can generate some code from a model, but that usually goes no further than the generation of some template code, where most of the work still has to be filled in by hand.

In contrast, MDA transformations are always executed by tools as shown in Figure 1-3. Many tools are able to transform a PSM into code; there is nothing new to that. Given the fact that the PSM is already very close to the code, this transformation isn't that exciting. What's new in MDA is that the transformation from PIM to PSM is automated as well. This is where the obvious benefits of MDA come in. How much effort has been spent in your projects with the painstaking task of building a database model from a high-level design? How much (precious) time was used by building a COM component model, or an EJB component model from that same design? It is indeed about time that the burden of IT-workers is eased by automating this part of their job.

At the time of writing, the MDA approach is very new. As a result of this, current tools are not sophisticated enough to provide the transformations from PIM to PSM and from PSM to code for one hundred percent. The developer needs to manually enhance the transformed PSM and/or code models. However, current tools are able to generate a running application from a PIM that provides basic functionality, like creating and changing objects in the system. This does allow a developer to have immediate feedback on the PIM that is under development, because a basic prototype of the resulting system can be generated on the fly.

Figure 1-3 *The three major steps in the MDA development process*

1.3 MDA BENEFITS

Let us now take a closer look at what application of MDA brings us in terms of improvement of the software development process.

1.3.1 Productivity

In MDA the focus for a developer shifts to the development of a PIM. The PSMs that are needed are generated by a transformation from PIM to PSM. Of course, someone still needs to define the exact transformation, which is a difficult and specialized task. But such a transformation only needs to be defined once and can then be applied in the development of many systems. The payback for the effort to define a transformation is large, but it can only be done by highly skilled people.

The majority of developers will focus on the development of PIMs. Since they can work independently of details and specifics of the target platforms, there is a lot of technical detail that they do not need to bother with. These technical details will be automatically added by the PIM to PSM transformation. This improves the productivity in two ways.

In the first place, the PIM developers have less work to do because platform-specific details need not be designed and written down; they are already addressed in the transformation definition. At the PSM and code level, there is much less code to be written, because a large amount of the code is already generated from the PIM.

The second improvement comes from the fact that the developers can shift focus from code to PIM, thus paying more attention to solving the business problem at hand. This results in a system that fits much better with the needs of the end users. The end users get better functionality in less time.

Such a productivity gain can only be reached by the use of tools that fully automate the generation of a PSM from a PIM. Note that this implies that much of the information about the application must be incorporated in the PIM and/or the generation tool. Because the high-level model is no longer "just paper," but directly related to the generated code, the demands on the completeness and consistency of the high-level model (PIM) are higher than in traditional development. A human reading a paper model may be forgiving—an automated transformation tool is not.

1.3.2 Portability

Within the MDA, portability is achieved by focusing on the development of PIMs, which are by definition platform independent. The same PIM can be automatically transformed into multiple PSMs for different platforms. Everything you specify at the PIM level is therefore completely portable.

The extent to which portability can be achieved depends on the automated transformation tools that are available. For popular platforms, a large number of tools will undoubtedly be (or become) available. For less popular platforms, you may have to use a tool that supports plug-in transformation definitions, and write the transformation definition yourself.

For new technologies and platforms that will arrive in the future, the software industry needs to deliver the corresponding transformations in time. This enables us to quickly deploy new systems with the new technology, based on our old and existing PIMs.

1.3.3 Interoperability

We have been incomplete regarding the overall MDA picture. As shown in Figure 1-4, multiple PSMs generated from one PIM may have relationships. In MDA these are called *bridges*. When PSMs are targeted at different platforms, they cannot directly talk with each other. One way or another, we need to transform concepts from one platform into concepts used in another platform. This is what interoperability is all about. MDA addresses this problem by generating not only the PSMs, but the necessary bridges between them as well.

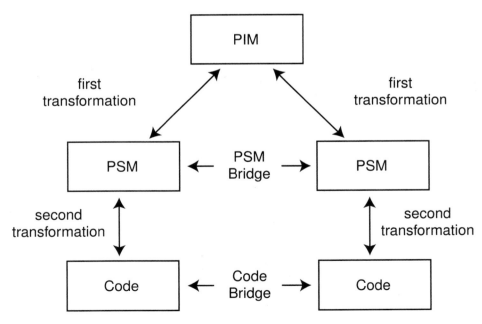

Figure 1-4 *MDA interoperability using bridges*

If we are able to transform one PIM into two PSMs targeted at two platforms, all of the information we need to bridge the gap between the two PSMs is available. For each element in one PSM we know from which element in the PIM it has been transformed. From the PIM element we know what the corresponding element is in the second PSM. We can therefore deduce how elements from one PSM relate to elements in the second PSM. Since we also know all the platform-specific technical details of both PSMs (otherwise we couldn't have performed the PIM-to-PSM transformations), we have all the information we need to generate a bridge between the two PSMs.

Take, for example, one PSM to be a Java (code) model and the other PSM to be a relational database model. For an element *Customer* in the PIM, we know to which Java class(es) this is transformed. We also know to which table(s) this *Customer* element is transformed. Building a bridge between a Java object in the Java-PSM and a table in the Relational-PSM is easy. To retrieve an object from the database, we query the table(s) transformed from *Customer,* and instantiate the class(es) in the other PSM with the data. To store an object, we find the data in the Java object and store it in the "Customer" tables.

Cross-platform interoperability can be realized by tools that not only generate PSMs, but the bridges between them, and possibly to other platforms, as well. You can "survive" technology changes while preserving your investment in the PIM.

1.3.4 Maintenance and Documentation

Working with the MDA life cycle, developers can focus on the PIM, which is at a higher level of abstraction than code. The PIM is used to generate the PSM, which in turn is used to generate the code. The model is an exact representation of the code. Thus, the PIM fulfills the function of high-level documentation that is needed for any software system.

The big difference is that the PIM is not abandoned after writing. Changes made to the system will eventually be made by changing the PIM and regenerating the PSM and the code. In practice today, many of the changes are made to the PSM and code is regenerated from there. Good tools, however, will be able to maintain the relationship between PIM and PSM, even when changes to the PSM are made. Changes in the PSM will thus be reflected in the PIM, and high-level documentation will remain consistent with the actual code.

In the MDA approach the documentation at a high level of abstraction will naturally be available. Even at that level, the need to write down additional information, which cannot be captured in a PIM, will remain. This includes, for example, argumentation for choices that have been made while developing the PIM.

1.4 MDA BUILDING BLOCKS

Now what do we need to implement the MDA process? The following are the building blocks of the MDA framework:

- High-level models, written in a standard, well-defined language, that are consistent, precise, and contain enough information on the system.
- One or more standard, well-defined languages to write high-level models.
- Definitions of how a PIM is transformed to a specific PSM that can be automatically executed. Some of these definitions will be "home-made," that is, made by the project that works according to the MDA process itself. Preferably, transformation definitions would be in the public domain, perhaps even standardized, and tunable to the individual needs of its users.
- A language in which to write these definitions. This language must be interpreted by the transformation tools, therefore it must be a formal language.
- Tools that implement the execution of the transformation definitions. Preferably these tools offer the users the flexibility to tune the transformation step to their specific needs.
- Tools that implement the execution of the transformation of a PSM to code.

At the time of writing, many of the above building blocks are still under development. Chapter 3 provides an overview of where we stand today.

In the following chapters each of the building blocks is further examined and we show how it fits into the overall MDA framework.

1.5 SUMMARY

The Model Driven Architecture is a framework for software development, defined by the OMG. Key to MDA is the importance of models in the software development process. Within MDA the software development process is driven by the activity of modeling your software system.

The MDA development life cycle is not very different from the traditional life cycle. The artifacts of the MDA are formal models, i.e., models that can be understood by computers. The following three models are at the core of the MDA:

- Platform Independent Model (PIM), a model with a high level of abstraction, that is independent of any implementation technology.

- Platform Specific Model (PSM), a model tailored to specify your system in terms of the implementation constructs that are available in one specific implementation technology. A PIM is transformed into one or more PSMs.
- Code, a description (specification) of the system in source code. Each PSM is transformed into code.

Traditionally the transformations from model to model, or from model to code, are done mainly by hand. In contrast, MDA transformations are always executed by tools. Many tools have been able to transform a PSM to code; there is nothing new to that. What's new in MDA is that the transformation from PIM to PSM is automated as well.

2

The MDA Framework

This chapter introduces the MDA framework that lies behind the process that we described in Chapter 1. The MDA framework consists of a number of elements that fit together in a specific way. A small and simple example is given to clarify the different elements.

2.1 WHAT IS A MODEL?

The name MDA stresses the fact that models are the focal point of MDA. The models we take into account are models that are relevant to developing software. Note that this includes more than just models of software. When a piece of software is meant to support a business, the business model is relevant as well.

But what exactly do we mean when we use the word *model*? To come up with a definition that is both general enough to fit many different types of models is difficult. The definition also needs to be specific enough to help us specify automatic transformation of one model into another. In the English dictionary we can find various meanings of model:

- The type of an appliance or of a commodity
- The example used by an artist
- A person posing for an artist
- A replica of an item built on a smaller scale, i.e., a miniature
- An example of a method of performing work
- An ideal used as an example
- The form of a piece of clothing or of a hairdo, and so on

What all of the above definitions have in common is that:

- A model is always an abstraction of something that exists in reality.

- A model is different from the thing it models, e.g., details are left out or its size is different.

- A model can be used as an example to produce something that exists in reality.

From these observations, it is apparent that we need a word to indicate "something that exists in reality.[1]" Because all of our models should be relevant in the context of software development, we use the word *system*. Most of the time the word system refers to a software system, but in the case of a business model, the business itself is the system.

Another observation we can make is that a model describes a system in such a way that it can be used to produce a similar system. The new system is not equal to the old one, because a model abstracts away from the details of the system; therefore, details in both old and new system might differ. Yet, because only the details are omitted in the model and the main characteristics remain, the newly produced system has the same main characteristics as the original, i.e., it is similar to it. The more detailed the model is, the more similar the systems it describes will be.

As we set out to find a definition to help us specify the automatic transformation of one model into another, it is clear that not all of the meanings in the dictionary are suitable for use within MDA. Obviously, we will not transform "a person posing for an artist" to another model.

A model is always written in a language. This might be UML, plain English, a programming language, or any other language we can think of. To enable automatic transformation of a model, we need to restrict the models suitable for MDA to models that are written in a well-defined language. A well-defined language has a well-defined form and meaning that can be interpreted automatically by a computer. We consider natural languages as not being well-defined, because they cannot be interpreted by computers. Therefore, they are not suitable for automatic transformations within the MDA framework. From this point onward we use the following definitions:

A model is a description of (part of) a system written in a well-defined language.

A well-defined language is a language with well-defined form (syntax), and meaning (semantics), which is suitable for automated interpretation by a computer.

---

1. Models themselves are also "things that exist in reality;" therefore, there are models of models. For sake of simplicity, this possibility is not addressed in this chapter. For more on this subject, see Chapter 11, "OMG Standards and Additional Technologies."

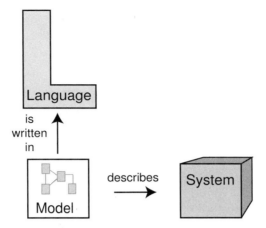

Figure 2-1 *Models and languages*

Note that although many of the example models in this book are written in UML, MDA is certainly not restricted to UML. The only restriction is that the models must be written in a language that is well-defined.

Our definition of model is a very general one. Although most people have a mental picture of a model as being a set of diagrams (as in UML), we do not put any restrictions on the way a model looks (the syntax) as long as it is well-defined. Our definition intentionally includes source code as a model of the software. Source code is written in a well-formed language, the programming language can be understood by a compiler, and it describes a system. It is, of course, a highly platform-specific model, but a model nevertheless. Figure 2-1 shows the relationship between a model, the system it describes, and the language in which it is written. We use the symbols from Figure 2-1 in the remainder of this book to distinguish between models and languages.

2.1.1 Relationships between Models

For a given system there can be many different models, that vary in the details that are, or are not, described. It is obvious that two models of the same system have a certain relationship. There are many types of relationships between models. For instance, one model may describe only part of the complete system, while another model describes another, possibly overlapping, part. One model may describe the system with more detail than another. One model may describe the system from a completely different angle than another.

Note that MDA focuses on one specific type of relationship between models: automatic generation of one model from another. This does not mean that the other types of relationships are less important. It only says that these relationships cannot (yet) be automated. For instance, adding attributes to a class and deciding what should be the types of these attributes is not a task that can be automated. It needs human intelligence.

2.2 TYPES OF MODELS

The definition of model given in section 2.1, What Is a Model?, is a very broad one that includes many different kind of models, so we will take a closer look at models. There are many ways to distinguish between types of models, each based on the answer to a question about the model:

- In what part of the software development process is the model used? Is it an analysis or design model?
- Does the model contain much detail? Is it abstract or detailed?
- What is the system that the model describes? Is it a business model or software model?
- What aspect of the system does the model describe? Is it a structural or dynamic model?
- Is the model targeted at a specific technology? Is it platform independent or platform specific?
- At which platform is the model targeted? Is it an EJB, ER, C++, XML, or other model?

What we need to establish is whether these distinctions are relevant in the context of model transformations. The answer to some of the above questions varies according to the circumstances. The distinction made is not a feature of the model itself. Whether a model is considered to be an analysis or design model depends not on the model itself, but on the interpretation of the analysis and design phases in a certain project. Whether a model is considered to be abstract or detailed depends on what is considered to be detail.

When the distinguishing feature is not a feature of the model itself, this feature is not a good indication for characterizing different types of models. So, answering the first two questions in the list above does not clearly distinguish different types of models. The answers to the other questions in the above list do indicate different types of models. We further investigate these distinctions in the following sections.

2.2.1 Business and Software Models

The system described by a business model is a business or a company (or part thereof). Languages that are used for business modeling contain a vocabulary that allows the modeler to specify business processes, stakeholders, departments, dependencies between processes, and so on.

A business model does not necessarily say anything about the software systems used within a company; therefore, it is also called a Computational Independent Model (CIM). Whenever a part of the business is supported by a software system, a specific software model for that system is written. This software model is a description of the software system. Business and software systems describe quite different categories of systems in the real world.

Still, the requirements of the software system are derived from the (part of the) business model that the software needs to support. For most business models there are multiple software systems with different software models. Each software system is used to support a different piece of one business model. So there is a relationship between a business model and the software models that describe the software supporting the business, as shown in Figure 2-2.

We have seen that the type of the system described by a model is relevant for model transformations. A CIM is a software independent model used to describe a business system. Certain parts of a CIM may be supported by software systems, but the CIM itself remains software independent. Automatic derivation of PIMs from a CIM is not possible, because the choices of what pieces of a CIM are to be supported by a software system are always human. For each system supporting part of a CIM, a PIM needs to be developed first.

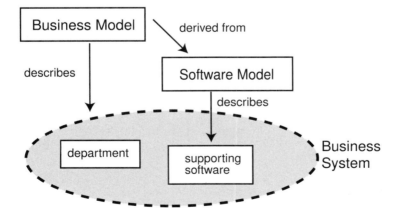

Figure 2-2 *Business and software models*

2.2.2 Structural and Dynamic Models

Many people talk about structural models versus dynamic models. In UML, for example, the class diagram is called a structural model and the state diagram a dynamic model, while in reality the class diagram and state diagram are so dependent on each other that they must be regarded as part of the same model.

The fact that we start software modeling by drawing classes in a class diagram doesn't mean we are developing a class model. We are developing a software model by defining static aspects through a static view. If we start our development by drawing a dynamic diagram, like the state or sequence diagram, we are developing a software model by defining dynamic aspects through a dynamic view. Later, when we add a state diagram to our class diagram, or a class diagram to our state diagram, we are merely adding dynamic aspects through a dynamic view to *the same model,* or vice versa. Therefore, the common terminology is a bit sloppy. The class and state diagrams could better be called structural and dynamic *views.* Figure 2-3 shows how different diagrams in UML are all views on the same model. They are all written in the same language: UML.

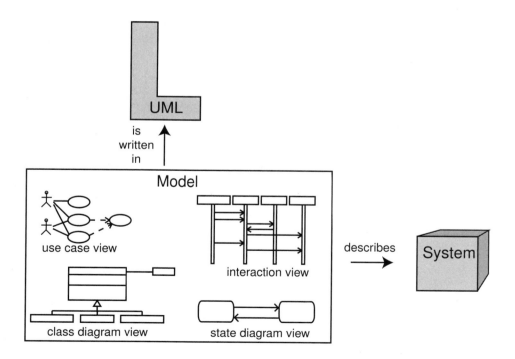

Figure 2-3 *Different views of one system in one model*

In UML the relationship between dynamic and static views is direct, because they show different visualizations of the same thing in the same model. For example, a class in a UML model is shown as a rectangle with the class name in a class view, while it is shown as the type of an instance in a sequence diagram. The same class can be the anchoring point for a complete state diagram. All the diagrams are views on the same class.

If a system has both structural *and* dynamic aspects and the language used is able to express both structural and dynamic aspects, the model of the system contains both aspects. Therefore, a UML model of a system includes both the structural and the dynamic aspects, shown in different diagrams.

If structural and dynamic aspects cannot be described in one model because the language used is not able to express certain aspects, there are indeed two models. Note that both models are related; they describe the same system. The type of the model is in such a case more clearly described by naming the language in which it is written than by the use of the connotation "structural" or "dynamic," e.g., an ER-model or Pet-

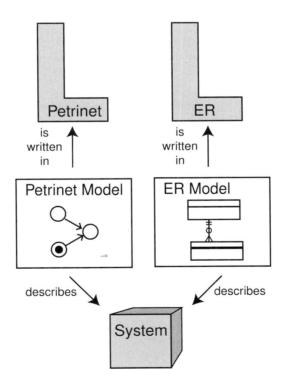

Figure 2-4 *Different models of one system written in different languages*

rinet-model. Figure 2-4 shows a situation where two different models describing the same system are written in two different languages.

We can conclude with the observation that the aspect that is described in a diagram or model (i.e., structural, dynamic) is not relevant for the type of a model. The essential characteristic of a model is the language in which the model is written. Some languages are more expressive than others and more suitable for representing certain aspects of a system.

2.2.3 Platform Independent and Platform Specific Models

The MDA standard defines the terms PIM and PSM. The OMG documentation describes this distinction as if this is a clear black-and-white issue. A model is always either a PIM or a PSM. In reality it is difficult to draw the line between platform independent and platform specific. Is a model written in UML specific for the Java platform because one of the class diagrams defines one or more interfaces? Is a model that describes the interactions of components specific for a certain platform only because some of the components are "legacy" components, which may be written in, let's say, COBOL? It is hard to tell.

The only thing one can say about different models is that one model is more (or less) platform specific than another. Within an MDA transformation, we transform a more platform independent model to a model that is more platform specific. Thus, the terms PIM and PSM are relative terms.

2.2.4 The Target Platforms of a Model

The last issue we need to analyze is whether the target platform is a relevant distinction between models in the context of model transformations. Is a design model in UML targeted at Smalltalk distinctively different from a design model in UML targeted at EJB? Yes, most people would say it is. But why? What is the difference?

The difference lies in the use of constructs (in UML) that can be easily mapped to one specific platform, but not to another. A model targeted at EJB has a different structure than a model targeted at Smalltalk. To generate these models from the same PIM we need different transformation rules.

Furthermore, the extent to which a model is platform specific is very important. Using UML profiles (see section 11.8, UML Profiles) a UML model can be made very specific for a certain platform. Such a model should be used as a PSM, not as a PIM. The transformation rules that take such a model as source are quite different from the rules that take a general UML/PIM model as the source.

We conclude that it is very important to know the target platform of a model and the degree to which the model is platform specific. For instance, a relational model targeted at SQL might be specific for a certain database vendor.

2.3 WHAT IS A TRANSFORMATION?

The MDA process, as described in section 1.2.1, shows the role that the various models, PIM, PSM, and code play within the MDA framework. A transformation tool takes a PIM and transforms it into a PSM. A second (or the same) transformation tool transforms the PSM to code. These transformations are essential in the MDA development process. In Figure 1-3 we have shown the transformation tool as a black box. It takes one model as input and produces a second model as its output.

When we open up the transformation tool and take a look inside, we can see what elements are involved in performing the transformation. Somewhere inside the tool there is a definition that describes how a model should be transformed. We call this definition the *transformation definition*. Figure 2-5 shows the structure of the opened up transformation tool.

Note that there is a distinction between the transformation itself, which is the process of generating a new model from another model, and the transformation definition. The transformation tool uses the same transformation definition for each transformation of any input model.

In order for the transformation specification to be applied over and over again, independent of the source model it is applied to, the transformation specification relates constructs from the source language to constructs in the target language. We can, for example, define a transformation definition from UML to C#, which describes which C# should be generated for a (or any!) UML model. This situation is depicted in Figure 2-6.

In general, we can say that a transformation definition consists of a collection of transformation rules, which are unambiguous specifications of the way that (a part of) one model can be used to create (a part of) another model. Based on these observations, we can now define transformation, transformation rule, and transformation definition.

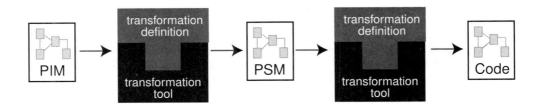

Figure 2-5 *Transformation definitions inside transformation tools*

Figure 2-6 *Transformation definitions are defined between languages*

> *A transformation is the automatic generation of a target model from a source model, according to a transformation definition.*
>
> *A transformation definition is a set of transformation rules that together describe how a model in the source language can be transformed into a model in the target language.*
>
> *A transformation rule is a description of how one or more constructs in the source language can be transformed into one or more constructs in the target language.*

To be useful at all, a transformation must have specific characteristics. The most important characteristic is that a transformation should preserve meaning between the source and the target model. Of course, the meaning of a model can only be preserved insofar as it can be expressed in both the source and the target model. For example, specification of behavior may be part of a UML model, but not of an Entity-Relationship (ER) model. Even so, the UML model may be transformed into an ER model, preserving the structural characteristics of the system only.

2.3.1 Transformations between Identical Languages

The definition above does not put any limitations on the source and target languages. This means that the source and target model may be written in either the same or in a different language. We can define transformations from a UML model to a UML model or from Java to Java.

There are several situations where this may occur. The technique of refactoring a model or a piece of code (remember code is also a model) can be described by a transformation definition between models in the same language. Another well-known example of a transformation definition is the normalization of an ER model. There are well-defined normalization rules that may be applied over and over again on different ER models with a determined outcome. For instance, the normalization rule that produces a model in the second normal form is:

▪ Shift all attributes in an entity that are not dependent on the complete key of that entity to a separate entity, holding a relationship between the original entity and the newly created one.

This rule may be applied to any ER model. It relates one entity and its attributes in the source model to two entities, their attributes, and a relationship in the target model, where both source and target model are written in the ER-modeling language.

In the case of transformations between UML models, we need to be very careful. Very often the purpose of the source and target models although both in UML, is completely different. In the examples in section 2.5, later in this chapter, we define a transformation from a PIM in UML to a PSM in UML. The trick is that the PSM is restricted to use only constructs from UML that can be mapped one-to-one onto constructs in the Java language. Conceptually, the target language is not plain UML, but a specific subset of UML, which we could call UML-for-Java. This kind of use of UML occurs often, and it is hard to recognize.

The UML-for-Java subset can be formalized by defining a UML profile for Java. Any UML profile in effect defines a completely *new language* which happens to be derived from the UML language. In Chapter 11 we elaborate on the role of UML profiles in MDA.

2.4 THE BASIC MDA FRAMEWORK

In the previous sections, we have seen the major elements that participate in the MDA framework: models, PIMs, PSMs, languages, transformations, transformation definitions, and tools that perform transformations. All of these elements fit together in the basic MDA framework, as depicted in Figure 2-7. Although most of the terms have been defined in the previous sections, we summarize of the elements and their role below:

▪ A *model* is a description of a system.

  ◆ A *PIM* is a Platform Independent Model, which describes a system without any knowledge of the final implementation platform.

  ◆ A *PSM* is a Platform Specific Model, which describes a system with full knowledge of the final implementation platform.

▪ A model is written in a well-defined *language*.

▪ A *transformation definition* describes how a model in a source language can be transformed into a model in a target language.

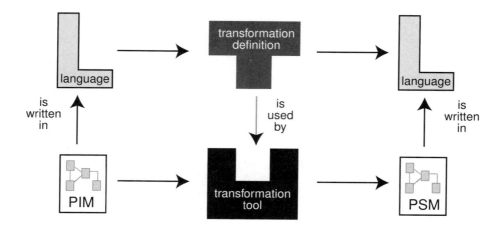

Figure 2-7 *Overview of the basic MDA framework*

- A *transformation tool* performs a transformation for a specific source model according to a transformation definition.

From the developer's point of view, the PSM and PIM are the most important elements. A developer puts his focus on developing a PIM, describing the software system at a high level of abstraction. In the next stage, he chooses one or more tools that are able to perform the transformation on the PIM that has been developed according to a certain transformation definition. This results in a PSM, which can then be transformed into code.

Note that the figure only shows one PSM, but that from one PIM often multiple PSMs and potential bridges between them are generated. The figure only shows one transformation between a PIM and a PSM, but another transformation to code is also necessary.

In sections 8.3.1 and 9.4 we complete the basic MDA framework with additional elements at the metalevel. These metalevels are explained in Chapter 8 and Chapter 9. Until Chapter 7, the framework as described in Figure 2-7 is sufficient.

2.5 EXAMPLES

In this section, we show two small examples of applying MDA. The examples themselves are not very complex, even rather trivial. These examples do not show the advantages of MDA. The purpose is to show how the MDA framework is applied in some concrete examples. In both examples we take a look at a high-level PIM mod-

```
┌────────────────────────────┐
│          Customer          │
├────────────────────────────┤
│ +title        : String     │
│ +name         : String     │
│ +dateOfBirth  : Date       │
├────────────────────────────┤
│                            │
└────────────────────────────┘
```

Figure 2-8 *Platform independent model*

eled in UML and a lower-level PSM for Java, also written in UML. Chapter 4 gives a more complex and realistic example.

2.5.1 Public and Private Attributes

In the first example we define a transformation between two UML models. The source model is a platform independent model, which is transformed into a lower level, more platform specific model for use with Java. The focus is on transforming public attributes into their respective get- and set-operations. One of the classes in the PIM is shown in Figure 2-8. The class *Customer* contains three attributes: *title, name,* and *dateOfBirth.* All attributes are declared public. In a high-level PIM it is normal to use public attributes. The meaning of a public attribute in a PIM is that the object has the specified property, and that this property can change value over time.

In the PSM, where we model the source code instead of the business concepts, the use of public attributes is considered to be bad design. It is better to apply information hiding techniques and encapsulate the public attributes as shown in Figure 2-9. All attributes are private and all access to the Customer is directed through well-defined operations. This allows the customer object to have control over its use and over its change of attributes.

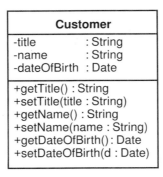

Figure 2-9 *Platform specific model targeted at Java*

Both PIM and PSM are useful, as they provide the right level of information to different types of developers and other stakeholders in the software development process. However, there is a clear relationship between the models. The transformation definition to transform the PIM into the PSM has several rules. The transformation rules are:

- For each class named *className* in the PIM there is a class named *className* in the PSM.

- For each public attribute named *attributeName : Type* of class *className* in the PIM the following attributes and operations are part of class *className* in the target model:
  - ◆ A private attribute with the same name: *attributeName : Type*
  - ◆ A public operation named with the attribute name preceded with "get" and the attribute type as return type: *getAttributeName() : Type*
  - ◆ A public operation named with the attribute name preceded with "set" and with the attribute as parameter and no return value: *setAttributeName(att : Type)*

This transformation rule has a reverse, a rule that transforms an aspect of the PSM into a PIM, which is formulated in the other direction:

- For each class named *className* in the PSM there is a class named *className* in the PIM.

- For each combination in the PSM of the following attributes and operations within the same class *className* a public attribute *attributeName : Type* should exist in the corresponding class *className* in the PIM
  - ◆ A private attribute named *attributeName : Type*
  - ◆ A public operation named: *getAttributeName() : Type*
  - ◆ A public operation named: *setAttributeName(att : Type)*

Because in this example we know that the targeted programming language is Java, we can write another transformation definition that transforms the PSM into source code. Combining and automating both transformations generates source code for the necessary operations, derived completely from the PIM.

2.5.2 Associations

We can extend the example above with more classes and associations between those classes. In Figure 2-10 the PIM is extended with two classes: *Order* and *Item*. The model shows that a customer may have multiple orders and each order may have one or more items. In the PSM, next to transforming the public attributes, we need to replace the associations by something that is directly mappable to the programming language. Naturally, for mapping associations with a multiplicity greater than one, we make use of the Java collection classes. The extra transformation rules are:

- For an association in the PIM, the following will be in the PSM:
  - For each association end there is a private attribute of the same name in the opposite class.
  - The type of this attribute is the class at the side of the association end if the multiplicity is zero or one, or the type is a *Set* if the multiplicity is larger than one.
  - The newly created attribute will have a corresponding *get* and *set* operation, following the same rules as other attributes.
- For a directed association the above is done only for the class from which the arrow points away.

The transformation that combines both the rules for public attributes and the rules for associations results in the PSM shown in Figure 2-11.

Looking at the PSM we see that the difference with the PIM is larger than in the first example. The associations between the classes are hard to find. If we only have the PSM at our disposal, we can deduce that *Order* has an association with *Customer*, because of the *customer* field. The multiplicity of the association must be zero or one. We cannot find whether this association is directed or not. The association between *Order* and *Item* is completely lost because in Java there is no restriction on the type of the elements that can be in the set *items* in *Order*, and *Item* does not contain any reference to *Order*. Defining a reverse transformation for the association transformation definition is basically impossible.

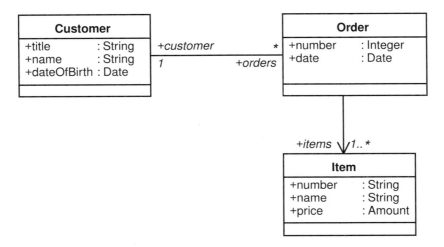

Figure 2-10 *Platform independent model, extended*

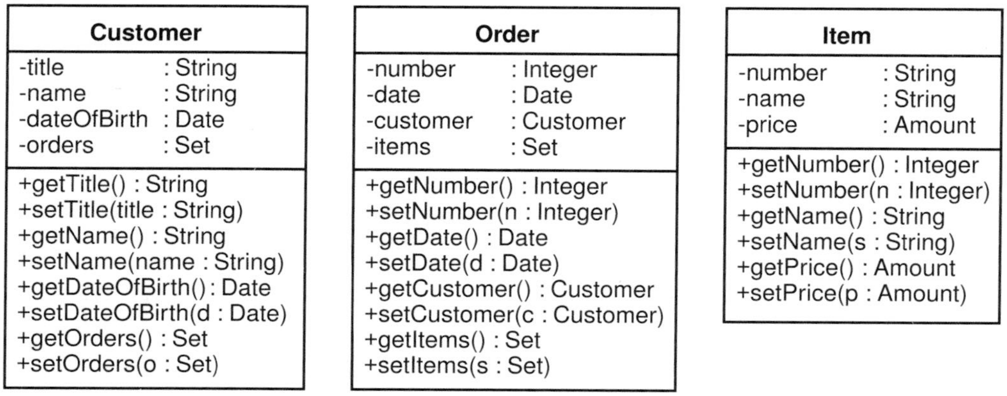

Customer		Order		Item	
-title	: String	-number	: Integer	-number	: String
-name	: String	-date	: Date	-name	: String
-dateOfBirth	: Date	-customer	: Customer	-price	: Amount
-orders	: Set	-items	: Set		
				+getNumber() : Integer	
+getTitle() : String		+getNumber() : Integer		+setNumber(n : Integer)	
+setTitle(title : String)		+setNumber(n : Integer)		+getName() : String	
+getName() : String		+getDate() : Date		+setName(s : String)	
+setName(name : String)		+setDate(d : Date)		+getPrice() : Amount	
+getDateOfBirth() : Date		+getCustomer() : Customer		+setPrice(p : Amount)	
+setDateOfBirth(d : Date)		+setCustomer(c : Customer)			
+getOrders() : Set		+getItems() : Set			
+setOrders(o : Set)		+setItems(s : Set)			

Figure 2-11 *Platform specific model, extended*

Note that in the transformation rule design decisions are written down. In the above rule we have chosen to have *set* operations for *Set*-type attributes that need a *Set* as parameter. This has resulted in the *setOrders(o : Set)* operation of Customer. An alternative would be to only have an *addOrder(o : Order)* operation. This makes addition of single orders easier. These choices are made by the person (or tool vendor) that specifies the transformation.

Often one would want to have explicit control over the transformation, e.g., stating that a certain association needs to be transformed to an attribute of type *HashSet* instead of *Set*, or that a certain association needs both operations *setOrders()* and *addOrder()*. We call this tuning of the transformation. Section 7.2 gives more information on this subject.

2.6 SUMMARY

In this chapter we have seen the MDA framework and the role that the different elements play within it:

- A *model* is a description of a system
  - A *PIM* is a Platform Independent Model, which describes a system without any knowledge of the final implementation platform.
  - A *PSM* is a Platform Specific Model, which describes a system with full knowledge of the final implementation platform.
- A model is written in a well-defined *language*.

- A *transformation definition* describes how a model in a source language can be transformed into a model in a target language.
- A *transformation tool* performs a transformation for a specific source model according to a transformation definition.

The framework is neutral with respect to the languages that are used to model or code a system. In practice, UML is the most widely used modeling language and probably will be for a while.

3

MDA Today

This chapter describes what has been achieved within the MDA at the time of writing. Hopefully, by the time you read this, the technology will have advanced somewhat further. This chapter gives an overview of the various OMG standards that can be used within the MDA, the tool support that you can expect, and development processes that you can use.

3.1 OMG STANDARDS

The MDA is defined and trademarked by the OMG. We therefore first take a look at the OMG standards that play a role within the MDA framework.

3.1.1 OMG Languages

The OMG defines a number of modeling languages that are suitable to write either PIMs or PSMs. The most well-known language is UML. This is the most widely used modeling language.

The Object Constraint Language (OCL) is a query and expression language for UML, which is an integral part of the UML standard. The term "Constraint" in the name is an unfortunate leftover from the time when OCL was used to specify only constraints to UML models. Currently, OCL is a full query language, comparable to SQL in its expressive power.

The Action Semantics (AS) for UML defines the semantics of behavioral models in UML. Unfortunately, it defines the behavior at a low-level foundation. Therefore, it is not directly suitable for writing PIMs. It lacks the higher level of abstraction that is necessary. The AS is not a language that can be used directly by a modeler, because it does not define a concrete syntax; you cannot write down anything at all in a standardized way.

UML includes a profile mechanism that enables us to define languages derived from the UML language. The language defined in the profile is a subset of UML with additional constraints and suitable for a specific use. It uses the UML diagrammatic notation and OCL textual queries, and looks like UML. Many such profiles are standardized by the OMG; others are not standardized, but publicly available. Official OMG profiles include the CORBA Profile, the Enterprise Distributed Object Computing (EDOC) Profile, the Enterprise Application Integration (EAI) Profile, and the Scheduling, Performance, and Time Profile. More profiles are being developed and will be standardized in the coming years. Profiles are usually suitable for writing PSMs.

The UML/EJB Mapping Specification (EJB01) is an example of a profile that is standardized through the Java Community Process. Several profiles for other programming languages, like Java, C#, and so on, are defined by individual organizations and tool vendors.

Another language that is defined by the OMG is the Common Warehouse Metamodel (CWM). This is a language specifically designed to model data mining and related systems.

Chapter 11 describes the various OMG languages and their role in MDA in more detail.

3.1.2 OMG Language and Transformation Definitions

Languages used within the MDA need to have formal definitions so that tools will be able to automatically transform the models written in those languages. All of the languages standardized by the OMG have such a formal definition. The OMG has a special language called the Meta Object Facility (MOF), which is used to define all other languages. This ensures that tools are able to read and write all languages standardized by the OMG.

The transformation definitions used in the MDA framework are currently defined in a completely nonstandardized way. To allow standardization of these transformation definitions, the OMG is currently working on a standard language to write transformation definitions. This standard is called QVT, which stands for Query, Views, and Transformations. At the time of writing, the Request for Proposals (RfP) for QVT has been published. QVT is still being worked on by OMG members so we don't yet know exactly how the finished specification will look.

3.2 UML AS PIM LANGUAGE

As seen in section 1.3.1 the level of completeness, consistency, and unambiguity of a PIM must be very high. Otherwise, it is not possible to generate a PSM from a PIM. Let's investigate to what extent UML is a good language for building PIMs.

3.2.1 Plain UML

The strongest point in UML is the modeling of the structural aspects of a system. This is mainly done through the use of class models, which enables us to generate a PSM with all structural features in place. The example in Chapter 4 shows how this is done.

UML has some weak points that stop us from generating a complete PSM from a PIM. The weak area in UML is in the behavioral or dynamic part. UML includes many different diagrams to model dynamics, but their definition is not formal and complete enough to enable the generation of a PSM. For example, what code (for any platform) would you generate from an interaction diagram, or from a use case?

Plain UML is suitable to build PIMs in which the structural aspects are important. When a PSM is generated, a lot of the work still remains to be done on the resulting model, to define the dynamic aspects of the system.

3.2.2 Executable UML

Executable UML (Mellor 2002) is defined as plain UML combined with the dynamic behavior of the Action Semantics (AS). The concrete syntax used in Executable UML has not been standardized.

The strength of plain UML, modeling the structural aspect, is present in Executable UML as well. Executable UML to some extent mends the weak point in plain UML, the modeling of behavior. In Executable UML the state machine becomes the anchor point for defining behavior. Each state is enhanced with a procedure written in the AS.

In principle, Executable UML is capable of specifying a PIM and generating a complete PSM, but there are a few problems:

- Relying on state machines to specify complete behavior is only useful in specific domains, especially embedded software development. In other, more administrative, domains the use of state machines to define all behavior is too cumbersome to be used in practice.

- The AS language is not a very high-level language. In fact, the concepts used are at the same abstraction level as a PSM. Therefore, using Executable UML has little advantage over writing the dynamics of the system in the PSM directly. You will have to write the same amount of code, at the same level of abstraction.

- The AS language does not have a standardized concrete syntax or notation; therefore, you cannot write anything in a standard way.

Executable UML is suitable within specialized domains, but even there the benefits might be less than you would expect, because of the low abstraction level of the action language.

3.2.3 UML–OCL Combination

Using the combination of UML with OCL to build a PIM allows for PIMs that have a high quality; that is, they are consistent, full of information, and precise. The strong structural aspect of UML can be utilized and made fully complete and consistent. Query operations can be defined completely by writing the body of the operation as an OCL expression. Business rules can be specified using OCL, including dynamic triggers.

The dynamics of the system can be expressed by pre- and post-conditions on operations. For relatively simple operations the body of the corresponding operation might be generated from the post-condition, but most of the time the body of the operation must be written in the PSM. In that case, generating code for the pre- and post-condition ensures that the code written in the PSM conforms to the required specification in the PIM.

Although the dynamics of the systems still cannot be fully specified in the UML–OCL combination, the combination of UML class models with OCL allows for a much more complete generation of PSMs and code than does plain UML. The use of the combination of UML and OCL is at the moment of this writing probably the best way to develop a high quality *and* high level PIM, because this results in precise, unambiguous, and consistent models that contain much information about the system to be implemented.

3.3 TOOLS

Ever since MDA became a popular buzzword, vendors have claimed that their tools support MDA. Tools that were on the market for many years, even before the name MDA was invented, make these claims. Most of these claims are true, in the sense that they support some aspect of MDA. We will use the MDA framework as shown in Figure 2-7 to analyze what level of support a tool really offers.

3.3.1 Support for Transformations

Support for MDA comes in many different varieties. Simple code generation from a model has been done for more than a decade, and lies well within the boundaries of MDA. The demands that MDA places on models and transformations of models in the ideal situation, however, are very high. In this section we will focus on the support for transformations that tools can offer.

PIM to PSM Transformation Tools

This type of tool transforms a high level PIM into one or more PSMs. This type of tool is barely available at the time of writing, although some tools offer minimal functionality in this area.

PSM to Code Transformation Tools

The most well-known support for MDA is given by tools that act as black-box PSM to code transformation tools. They have a built-in transformation definition and take one predefined type of model as source and produce another predefined type as target. The source model is a PSM, while the target is the code model. In fact, code generation from traditional CASE tools follows this pattern.

Several tools persist the relationship between the PSM and code, and enable you to see changes in either of the models reflected in the other model immediately after the change. This is possible because of the fact that the PSM and code are relatively close to each other, and have almost the same level of abstraction.

PIM to Code Transformation Tools

Another type of tool supports both the PIM to PSM and the PSM to code transformation. Sometimes the user will only see a direct PIM to code transformation and the PSM is left implicit. With this type of tool, the source and target language and the transformation definition are built into the tool that acts as a black box.

UML is usually used as the PIM language. Dynamic functionality that cannot be expressed in UML needs to be added manually in the generated code.

Tunable Transformation Tools

Tools should allow for some tuning or parameterization of a transformation. Access to the transformation definition to adjust it to your own requirements is usually not available. The best one can get today is a transformation definition written in an internal tool-specific scripting language. It is a time-consuming task to make changes to such a script. Because there is no standard language to write transformation definitions yet (see QVT in section 3.1.2), transformation definitions are by definition tool-specific.

Most tools only work for a predefined PIM language, which is often required to be a restricted variant of UML. Although UML diagrams are used to model a PIM, internally the tools do not use the UML language definition, but their own tool-specific definition of UML. Because this does not always follow the UML language definition, even UML experts will have to learn the tool-specific UML definition first and will have difficulty writing transformation definitions.

Transformation Definition Tools

Transformation definition tools support the creation and modification of transformation definitions. This type of tool is needed when you cannot use a transformation definition off the shelf and need to create your own transformation definitions. The only type of transformation definition tool that we have encountered are the tool-specific scripting languages described in the previous paragraph. The heavy dependency of MDA on complex transformation definitions drives a need for a transformation definition language (QVT) and tools that are better suited to this task. More flexible tools should allow a new language definition to be plugged in and used in a transformation. Such tools are not on the market yet.

Because the tools that we have at our disposal today are not ideal, you might conclude that you cannot use MDA successfully today. The situation is far better than that. Although the full potential of MDA might not yet be achievable, the tools we have today can give us enough of the MDA benefits to be useful.

3.3.2 Categorizing Tools

Although transformation tools are at the very heart of an MDA development environment, they are not the only tools that are needed. Next to the functionality that transformation tools bring, other functionality is relevant. For instance, one needs a tool in

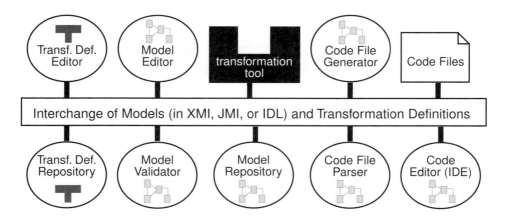

Figure 3-1 *Functionality in an MDA development environment*

which models can be made and changed. In Figure 3-1 the functionality that we need in the complete environment is shown. We will explain each item in more detail.

- Code Editor (IDE): The common functions that are provided by an Interactive Development Environment (IDE), for example, debugging, compilation, and code editing, cannot be missed.
- Code Files: Although we can consider code to be a model, it is usually kept in the form of text-based files. Text-based files are not the format that other "tools" are able to understand. Therefore, we need the following two items:
  - Code File Parser: A parser that reads a text-based code file and stores the code in the model repository in a model-based form that other tools can use.
  - Code File Generator: A generator that reads the code in the model repository and produces a text-based code file.
- Model Repository: The "database" for models, where models are stored and can be queried using XMI, JMI, or IDL (see section 11.2.1).
- Model Editor (CASE tool): An editor for models, in which models can be constructed and modified.
- Model Validator: Models used for generation of other models must be extremely well-defined. Validators can check models against a set of (predefined or user-defined) rules to ensure that the model is suitable for use in a transformation.
- Transformation Definition Editor: An editor for transformation definitions, in which transformation definitions can be constructed and modified.
- Transformation Definition Repository: The storage for transformation definitions.

Most of today's tools combine a number of functions in a more or less open fashion. The traditional CASE tools provide a model editor and a model repository. A code generator based on a scripting language and plugged into a CASE tool provides the transformation tool and transformation definition editor. In that case, the transformation repository is simply text files.

All functions may come in two forms: language specific or generic. A language-specific tool may, for example, provide a model editor for UML and a code generator from UML to C# only. A generic model editor would enable the user to edit any model, as long as a language definition is available.

Selecting Tools

If you are selecting tools to set up your MDA development environment, the above features can help to find your way among the myriad of tools available. First of all you need to find out your own requirements. Are you happy to be language specific, do you want to be able to combine different tools using standardized interfaces, or are you happy with one monolithic tool that incorporates all the functionality you need?

From the tool perspective, you can investigate what functions are supported by a tool and how language specific they are. You should also check whether the functions, the complete tool, or both, can work on models that are interchanged using standard mechanisms (XMI, JMI, IDL). When you go through all of the potential functions, you are able to get a good characterization of the tool in question. There are no tools that provide all functionality in a fully generic way; therefore, you should be prepared to choose several tools that need to be combined.

Although transformations are at the core of MDA, many tools that claim to support MDA do not perform transformations. Instead, they provide some of the other functionality that is required in an MDA development environment. For instance, a tool may only implement the model repository functionality. This is perfectly all right, because you will need to combine multiple tools anyway. The main issue is to find out what features a specific tool supports.

We have not included a tool comparison in this book because the tool market around MDA is still in flux. As the MDA further evolves, tools will start to support pieces of the MDA process. Any characterization of existing tools will be outdated by the time you are reading this. You are much better off applying the above categorization to tools that you encounter yourself. References to tools that claim MDA support can be found at the OMG website: http://www.omg.org/mda.

3.4 DEVELOPMENT PROCESSES

The MDA does not require a specific process to be used for software development. Processes are not standardized by the OMG, so you are free to choose your own. Of course, the central position of models and transformations in MDA should be reflected in such a process. We will take a short look at some of the more popular processes and show how they can be used for MDA development.

3.4.1 Agile Software Development

A current trend in the software development process is to minimize the amount of effort and time spent in building models that will only serve as documentation, even though they do capture some of the interesting aspects of the software to be built. The purpose is to ensure that software is delivered that works for the users. Since requirements continuously change, the software that is being developed must change accordingly. The ability for a software project to accommodate changes in a flexible and immediate way is the core aspect of Agile Software Development. According to Cockburn (2002), "Working software is valued over comprehensive documentation." Well, we couldn't agree more. At the Web site http://agilemanifesto.org you can find the

Agile Manifesto describing the agile principles. On this website you may post a quote why you like this approach. The quote from one of the authors of this book is:

> As co-author of the UML standard, people usually think I love large and detailed models. The contrary is true, a model is only worth building if it directly helps to achieve the final goal: building a working system. With the emergence of MDA tools, it becomes possible to directly move from model to code. This "promotes" models from being merely documentation to becoming part of the delivered software, just like the source code.

Because changing a model means changing the software, the MDA approach helps support agile software development.

3.4.2 Extreme Programming

The XP approach is a very popular way of working, where the focus lies on writing code in small increments, such that you have a working system all the time. Each new requirement must be accompanied by an explicit test case, which is used to test the software. When adding new functionality, all previous tests are run in addition to the new tests, to ensure that existing functionality is not broken.

As we explained in section 1.1.1, the focus on code only is too limited. Code must be augmented with so-called "markers" that document the code at a higher level. In extreme programming this is often seen as overhead. When we realize that these markers may take the form of MDA models that directly transform into code, creating these markers is not overhead anymore. On the contrary, the high-level models help to develop the software faster.

This means that we can bring XP to a higher abstraction level, and we might want to talk about "Extreme Modeling."

3.4.3 Rational Unified Process (RUP)

The RUP is a process that is much more elaborate, or much heavier, than the agile or extreme processes. Project managers often like these larger and more structured processes because they give a better feeling of control over the project. Especially for large projects, it is clear that a more elaborate process than extreme programming is needed. On the other hand, many people consider the RUP process as being too large and unwieldy, favoring bureaucratic development of large stacks of paper over "real" software development, i.e., writing code.

UML plays an important role within RUP. Many of the artifacts in RUP take the form of some UML model. If we are able to use these models in an MDA fashion, they can be used to generate PSMs and code. When we configure RUP for an MDA project, we need to make sure that the models that we produce fulfill the requirements that MDA puts on them.

When we do this, the models used in RUP are no longer bureaucratic overhead; they become "real" software development. The balance between writing paper documents and developing code moves more into the direction of developing code. At the same time, the artifacts that are produced will satisfy project managers in their quest for keeping control.

3.5 SUMMARY

In this chapter we have seen that the MDA framework can be populated by a number of different OMG standards. At the same time standards like the MOF and UML profiles allow non-OMG organizations to develop their own standards that will fit seamlessly in the MDA framework.

Tools are of great importance to the success of MDA. A wide spectrum of functionality is needed in an MDA environment, including traditional tools. Each tool may provide some or more of the functionality needed, and there are standardized ways that tools can communicate with each other.

Note that MDA is an emerging technology that is still in its infancy. Neither the languages nor the tools are developed enough to achieve the hundred percent code generation that is promised by MDA. There is always a need for manual change within the generated code. However, tools can provide enough functionality to make a significant impact on your software development process.

MDA can be used in existing software development processes. What is needed is more focus on the models that are developed to ensure that they are complete and consistent enough to be used in MDA transformations.

In Chapter 12 we take a look at the promise that MDA brings us. When the languages and tools become more mature, MDA has the ability to become a major paradigm shift in the software development community.

Rosa's Application of MDA

Together with the next two chapters, this chapter gives a concrete example of the MDA process. In order to show the power of the MDA approach, the system described is not trivial. It is not a toy system, but a real-life example. We will demonstrate how a fairly simple PIM is transformed automatically into rather complex PSMs and code. The complexity of the complete example is considerable. However, the example is not completely detailed out in all parts of the system in order to limit the size of this book. In this chapter the requirements of the example system are stated and an overview is given of the models and transformations involved.

If you are confident that you completely understand the concepts from the earlier chapters, then you may skip the following three chapters, and go directly to Chapter 7.

4.1 ROSA'S BREAKFAST SERVICE

The example we will be exploring in this book is the ordering system for Rosa's Breakfast Service. The example system described in this and subsequent chapters is implemented using the OptimalJ tool. You can download OptimalJ and the example at the Web site http://www.klasse.nl/mdaexplained.

4.1.1 The Business

Rosa has founded a company that supplies a complete breakfast delivered to the homes of its customers. Customers can order from one of the breakfast menus on Rosa's Web site, indicate the hour and place of delivery, give their credit card number, and the ordered breakfast will be delivered. Rosa's slogan is: "Surprise your husband, wife, lover, valentine, mother, father, or friend on their special day while still enjoying the comfort of your bed."

Rosa has composed a series of breakfasts, each of which comes with special decorations. For instance, the Valentine breakfast is served on plates decorated with small hearts and cupids, with matching napkins. The items served are set by the choice of breakfast. For instance, if you choose the French breakfast, you will get one cup of coffee, one glass of orange juice, two croissants and one roll, butter, and jam. But if you choose the English breakfast, you will get two fried eggs and bacon, three pieces of toast, marmalade, and a pot of tea. The Champagne Feast breakfast, which always serves two persons, includes a bottle of champagne, four baguettes, a choice of french cheese and pâtés, and a thermos bottle filled with coffee (to sober up afterwards). Orders can be filled for any number of people, where any in the party may order a different breakfast.

The items served are set, but customers can indicate the style in which the breakfast is served. They can choose between *simple*, *grand*, and *deluxe*. A *simple* breakfast is served on a plastic tray with carton plates and paper napkins. The orange juice glass, when included, is made of plastic, too. A *grand* breakfast is served on a wooden tray with pottery plates and cups, and simple white cotton napkins, and the glass is made of real glass. A *deluxe* breakfast is served on a silver tray with a small vase with some flowers. The plates are fine pottery plates and the napkins are decorated, made from the finest linen. Obviously, the price of the breakfast is higher when the serving style is better. Some breakfast types, like the Champagne Feast, can be ordered in the grand or deluxe style only.

Rosa has ten employees that come in her kitchen at half past five in the morning and work until noon. Five of them take care of deliveries, and five do the cooking and preparation of the breakfasts. Rosa's kitchen is located next to a bakery. The first thing Rosa does in the morning is get fresh bread from the bakery. All other ingredients are kept in supply. Twice a week their inventory is resupplied.

Rosa wants to give her customers a bit of flexibility. Customers may, after choosing a standard breakfast as basis, decide to put in extra comestibles, alter the amount of certain parts, and even remove parts from the breakfast. So, if you like the Champagne Feast breakfast, you may order two bottles of champagne instead of one, add another baguette, and leave out the smelly cheese and the coffee (coffee won't help after two whole bottles of champagne anyhow).

4.1.2 The Software System

In this example we are not very interested in the delicious breakfasts Rosa makes; instead, we look at the system needed to support Rosa's business. The ordering system is a standard Web-based, three-tier application. There will be two different Web interfaces, one for the customers, and one for Rosa's employees to indicate which breakfasts they need to make and deliver. If the customer agrees, his or her name and address will be kept in the system. This will enable Rosa to give a discount to regular customers.

The customer Web interface must respond to the customer information. When a known customer logs in, a list of previous orders must be shown with the option to repeat that order. The database should hold customer information: the name, price, and contents of all breakfast types offered, and the ordering information. The middle-tier will primarily add orders and customers to the database.

We have decided to use a three-tier architecture for Rosa's system. Of course, other choices could be made, and the decision on what architecture to use must be made carefully, but that is not the subject of this book. The three-tier application will consist of a database, a middle tier using Enterprise Java Beans (EJB), and a user interface built with Java Server Pages (JSP).

4.2 APPLYING THE MDA FRAMEWORK

Rosa will be interested only in the final system. But, because this is an example of how the MDA framework can be applied, we are interested in the process of building Rosa's Breakfast System. We will dissect this process into parts that have meaning within the MDA framework. We must identify which PSMs and code models should be delivered and which transformation definitions should be used to generate the PSMs and code models. All elements of the MDA framework used in this example are shown in Figure 4-1. The models are shown as rectangles and the transformations are shown as arrows.

4.2.1 The PIM and PSMs

To start the MDA process we need to build a platform-independent model that comprises the whole of Rosa's business. For the sake of simplicity, our PIM will be written in plain UML. This is the only model that the developer will create completely "by hand." The other models are mostly generated.

Because each tier is implemented using a different technology, we need three PSMs, one for each tier. The first PSM specifies the database, and is described by a relational model depicted in an Entity-Relationship diagram.

The PSM for the middle tier, which we call the EJB model, is written in a language that is a UML variant. It uses classes, associations, and so on, as in UML, but there are a number of stereotypes defined explicitly for the EJB platform.

The PSM for the Web interface is also written in a UML variant. This language uses different stereotypes than the UML variant used for the EJB model. Neither UML variant is standardized as a profile. They are small and simple, so we will not give an explanation of these UML variants.

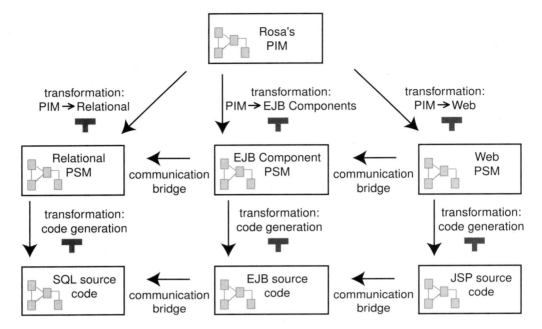

Figure 4-1 *Three levels of models for Rosa's Breakfast Service*

4.2.2 The PIM to PSM Transformations

Because three PSMs need to be generated, we need three PIM to PSM transformations:

- A PIM to Relational model transformation: a transformation that takes as input a model written in UML and produces a model written in terms of Entity-Relationship diagrams.

- A PIM to EJB model transformation: a transformation that takes as input a model written in UML and produces a model written in a UML variant using special EJB stereotypes.

- A PIM to Web model transformation: a transformation that takes as input a model written in UML and produces a model written in a UML variant using special stereotypes for the Web interface.

4.2.3 The PSM to Code Model Transformations

For each PSM, we need to generate code. Note that in Chapter 2, The MDA Framework, code was explicitly included to fit in our definition of model. Therefore, we can speak of code models written in some programming language. The code model defines the application in code. For Rosa's business we will have three code models in SQL, Java, and JSP, respectively. Therefore, we need three PSM to code transformations:

- A relational model to SQL transformation: a transformation that takes as input a model written as an Entity-Relationship model and produces a model written in SQL.

- An EJB model to Java transformation: a transformation that takes as input a model written in the UML EJB variant and produces a model written in Java.

- A Web model to JSP and HTML transformation: a transformation that takes as input a model written in the UML Web variant and produces a model written in JSP and HTML.

4.2.4 Three Levels of Abstraction

All models in this example describe or specify the same system, although at a different level of abstraction.

- At the highest level of abstraction we define the PIM. This model defines the concepts without any specific technology detail.

- At the next level there are the PSMs. These models abstract away from coding patterns in the technologies, but still they are platform specific.

- At the lowest level there are the three code models. These models are, of course, pure platform specific models.

Figure 4-1 shows the different models at the three levels of abstraction and the transformations between them. Note that the three tiers and the three levels of abstraction are orthogonal. The levels of abstraction are depicted from top to bottom; the tiers are depicted from right to left.

The following two chapters address the transformations and technologies needed to generate the PSMs and code models. Chapter 5 describes the transformation to the three PSMs and Chapter 6 explains portions of the code models of Rosa's Breakfast Service.

4.3 The PIM in Detail

The PIM for Rosa's Breakfast System is depicted in Figure 4-2. The PIM is the only model that must be created by humans in a creative process. To find out how to build such a model you can read a large number of books on UML and modeling. Here we assume that the creative process has been successfully completed with the PIM in Figure 4-2 as the result.

In the PIM every standard breakfast contains a number of parts; each part indicates the amount in which a certain comestible is present in the breakfast. Every order consists of a number of breakfasts. The price of each breakfast is determined based on the chosen style and the price of the chosen standard breakfast. The price of the order is simply the addition of the prices of all breakfasts plus a small delivery fee.

The model in Figure 4-2 defines the breakfast services independently from any specific technology, so indeed, it is a PIM. But Rosa does not want a model, she wants a running system. Therefore, we need to transform the PIM into a number of PSMs, taking into account the relationships between these PSMs.

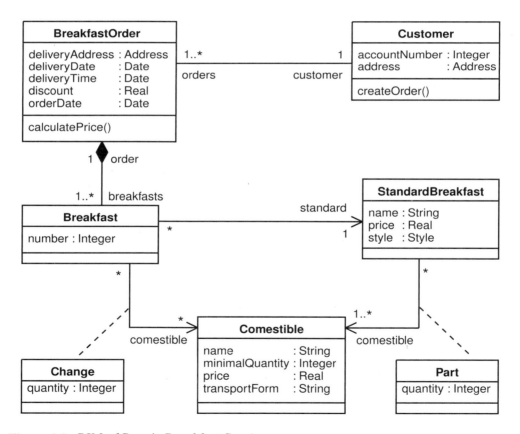

Figure 4-2 *PIM of Rosa's Breakfast Service*

4.4 SUMMARY

In order to show the power of the MDA approach, an example system is described that is not trivial. The example is a system that supports Rosa's Breakfast Service, a company that supplies a complete breakfast delivered to the homes of its customers.

A fairly simple PIM specifying the system is described. This PIM will be automatically transformed into a Relational PSM, a Web PSM, and an EJB PSM. The three PSMs will then be transformed into three separate code models. The next two chapters describe the transformations to be performed.

5

Rosa's PIM to Three PSMs

This chapter gives insight into the three PIM to PSM transformations that are needed to implement the system for Rosa's Breakfast Service.

5.1 THE PIM TO RELATIONAL TRANSFORMATION

The transformation rules for generating relational database models typically take care of a consistent object-relational mapping. Although most of these rules are rather straightforward and well-known (Blaha 1998), it can be a hard job to execute them manually. Small changes in the PIM can have a large effect on the relational model. For instance, changing the type of an attribute in the PIM from a simple data type to a class means introducing a foreign key in the corresponding table. The simple data type can be mapped directly to a column in a table. But if the data type is a class, this class will be mapped to a table itself. The column will now have to hold a reference (foreign key) to a key value in that other table.

What rules should be used to generate a relational model? Note that we want to formulate rules that will apply to any UML model, not only to Rosa's PIM. First, we must decide how the basic data types are being mapped. This is a fairly simple task. All we need to do is find the right corresponding data type in the relational model. Data types can be mapped according to the following rules. Note that we define an arbitrary length for each of the relational data types.

- A UML string will be mapped onto a SQL VARCHAR(40).
- A UML integer will be mapped onto an INTEGER.
- A UML date will be mapped onto a DATE.

But what do we with the Address? In the PIM the address is not a class, but a data type, a struct containing only attributes, and no operations. We have two options: either make a separate table for every data type, or inline the data type into the table that holds the attribute. Here we choose the latter option, because it will simplify the alignment with the EJB model. So for struct data types we have the following rule:

- A UML data type that has no operations will be mapped onto a number of columns, each representing a field in the data type.

Second, every class should be transformed into a table, where all attributes are fields in the table (rules ClassToTable and AttrToCol). When the type of the attribute is not a data type but a class, the field in the table should hold a foreign key to the table representing that class (rule AttrToFrkey). Note that we do not yet take into account the possibility that the multiplicity of the attribute is more than one.

The third step is more complicated. Associations in the UML model need to be transformed into a foreign key relation in the database model, possibly introducing a new table. Note that we have several possibilities for the multiplicities of an association from class A to class B in a UML model:

- The multiplicity at A is zero-or-one.
- The multiplicity at A is one.

or

- The multiplicity at A is more than one.

The same holds for the multiplicity at B. This leaves us with nine different combinations of multiplicities at both ends. Furthermore, we have to take into account that an association can be adorned with an association class. The rule can best be expressed in pseudocode:

```
if the association A to B is adorned by an association class
    or the multiplicity at both ends is more-than-one
then create a table representing the association class or the
        association
        and create foreign keys in both the table representing A and
        the table representing B referring this new table
else if the multiplicity at one end is zero-or-one
    then create a foreign key in the table representing the class
            at that end, referencing the other end
    else /* the multiplicity of the association is one-to-one */
        create a foreign key in one of the tables, referencing the
        other end
    endif
endif
```

Note that in this example we do not take into account the navigability of the association. We assume, for the sake of simplicity, that all associations are navigable.

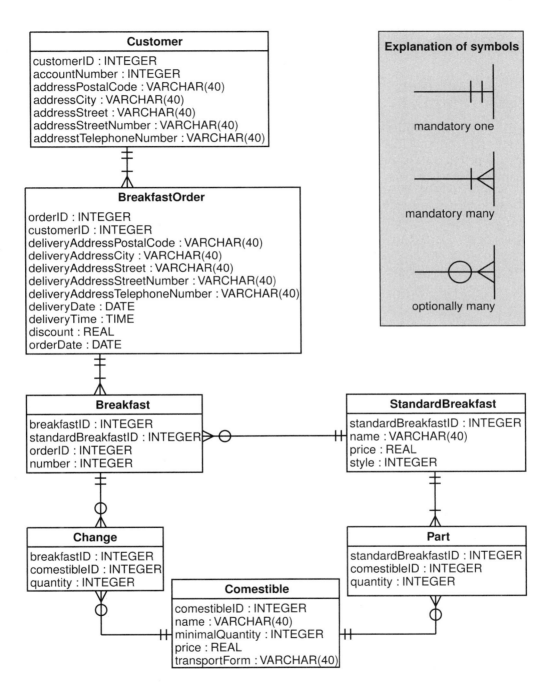

Figure 5-1 *Relational PSM of Rosa's Breakfast Service*

Each column in a relational model may or may not have the NULL value. In this transformation, only the columns generated from the attributes of the PIM may have the value NULL. The other columns are generated based on the association ends to constitute the foreign keys. These columns may not have the value NULL. The following rules correspond with the above:

- A UML attribute will be mapped to a column that may contain the NULL value.
- A UML association end will be mapped to a number of columns that may not contain the NULL value.

Figure 5-1 depicts the resulting database model in the form of an Entity-Relationship diagram. You can see that there is one table for each class in the PIM. Columns that are part of the key are repeated as foreign key columns in tables representing the "many" side of the association. The struct called *address* is inlined into the Customer and BreakfastOrder tables, and for each field there is one column in the table. The fact that a column may have the NULL value is not shown in the diagram, but assumed to be part of the generated relational model.

5.2 THE PIM TO EJB TRANSFORMATION

To complete the system for Rosa's Breakfast Service we need to generate an EJB PSM. We will make a number of architectural choices in the way that we use the EJB framework. These choices are specific for Rosa's Breakfast Service. Depending on the project requirements and the possibilities offered by the available tools, you will need to make your own choices in your own situation. We start out by explaining some aspects of the choices we have made regarding the EJB PSM.

5.2.1 A Coarse Grained EJB Model

The EJB model for Rosa's Breakfast Service is structured in a rather different manner than the PIM. We could have built a component model for Rosa's Breakfast Service by simply generating a component for each class. However, it is crucial for the performance of EJB components in a distributed environment with remote access that the communication between components remains minimal.

The attributes of an object could be exchanged one by one, where each get- or set-operation on an attribute value causes a remote method invocation. This is a straightforward, but rather naive approach. To minimize the frequency of interaction between components, wherever possible, it is better to exchange all attributes of an object in one remote call. This results in messages that are more complex, and include a relatively high amount of data, and in component interfaces that have a relatively low number of operations, relieving the burden on the communication network.

Furthermore, it is better to keep the number of components relatively small, because intercomponent communication will not burden the network, whereas intracomponent communication will. To minimize the number of components, we can combine closely related classes into one component, instead of having a component for each of them separately. We call a component model that adheres to these principles a coarse grained component model.

> *A coarse grained component model is a model of components where the components are large and have infrequent interaction with a relatively high amount of data in each interaction.*

In contrast to the coarse grained component model there is the fine grained component model.

> *A fine grained component model is a model of components where the components are small and have frequent communication with a low amount of data in each interaction.*

For Rosa's Breakfast Service we have chosen to use a coarse grained EJB component model. There are a number of books where you can find out more about component models (for example, Cheeseman 2001, Szyperski 1998, and Allen 1998). This book does not address that subject.

The interfaces of the coarse grained components have methods to exchange complete sets of associated objects, and they do not have methods for accessing the individual attributes and associations between these objects. Therefore, a number of classes in the source model must be clustered into so-called *EJB data schemas*.

> *An EJB data schema is a set of classes, attributes, and associations that is served by an EJB component as a whole.*

> *An EJB data class is a class that is part of an EJB data schema.*

To find out which EJB data classes should be part of a data schema, we use the *composite aggregation* property of the associations in the PIM. Every class that is part of a whole is clustered into the data schema that is generated from the whole. For example, the class *Breakfast* is defined to be part of the class *BreakfastOrder*, therefore Breakfast will be clustered in the data schema for *BreakfastOrder* and there will be no separate data schema or component for *Breakfast*.

Likewise, association classes are clustered in the data schema that is generated from the associated class that is able to navigate to the other associated class. For example, the class *Change* would be clustered into the data schema for *Breakfast*, but because the class *Breakfast* itself is clustered into the data schema for *BreakfastOrder*, the class *Change* becomes part of the data schema for *BreakfastOrder* as well.

A client of the EJB component can access the details of these clustered classes by getting a so-called *EJB data object*.

> **An EJB data object is an instance of an EJB data class.**

Each data class has its own local get- and set-operations for its attributes and associations to other data classes. When the client of the EJB component has finished, all changes that need to be made on the data objects are sent back to the EJB component with the request to process all changes.

Besides data classes that are holding the state of the exchanged objects, we need so-called *key classes*.

> **An EJB key class is a class that holds the data that is needed to identify EJB data objects.**

If a data class has an association to a class that does not reside in the same data schema, it will refer to a *key class* instead of a data class. In this manner, the amount of exchanged data in one data object is limited to the instances of the classes within one *data schema*.

5.2.2 The Transformation Rules

Now that we have established that we are going to generate a coarse grained EJB model, we are able to define the rules for the transformation from the PIM to the EJB PSM. Figure 5-2 shows the four EJB components that result from this transformation.

As explained in the previous section, the granularity of the EJB components is based on the composition of the classes in the domain model. In the transformation rules, we will use the term *outermost composition of x* to refer to the class that is not a part (via a composite association) of another class and is equal to or the (direct or indirect) container of the class *x*. To make the following transformation rules readable, we will leave out the words *UML* and *EJB* whenever the source and target model are clear.

1. For each PIM class, an EJB key class is generated.

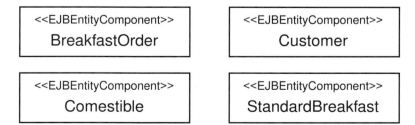

Figure 5-2 *Top-level EJB component model for Rosa's system*

2. Each PIM class that is not a composite part of another PIM class is transformed into an EJB component and an EJB data schema.

3. Each PIM class is transformed into an EJB data class residing in an EJB data schema that is generated from the PIM class that is the outermost composition of the transformed PIM class.

4. Each PIM association is transformed into an EJB association within an EJB data schema that is generated from the PIM class that is the outer-most composition of the transformed PIM association.

5. Each PIM association class is transformed into two EJB associations and an EJB data class. The EJB associations and the EJB data class are generated within the EJB data schema that is generated from the PIM class that is the outer-most composition of the PIM class that can navigate across the transformed PIM association class.

6. Each PIM attribute of a class is transformed into an EJB attribute of the mapped EJB data class.

7. Each PIM operation is transformed into an EJB operation of the generated EJB component that is generated from the PIM class that is the outer-most composition of the PIM class that owns the transformed PIM operation.

Figure 5-3 depicts the EJB data schemas of the *Comestible* and *StandardBreakfast* components. As indicated by the composition relations between the classes in the PIM, the *Comestible* data schema includes only the *Comestible* EJB data class, while the *StandardBreakfast* data schema includes the EJB data classes *StandardBreakfast* and *Part*.

5.3 THE PIM TO WEB TRANSFORMATION

The Web model specifies the definitions of the Web components. The Web components serve HTML content to the user. Each component serves a subset of the classes and associations of the system. Extra details are added to the Web model to define the layout and the user interactions of the HTML pages. In this example, the Web components serve the same classes as in the data schemas of the entity beans.

Web components are defined similarly to EJB components. The served classes and associations are defined in Web data schemas similar to the EJB data schemas. The most important differences are:

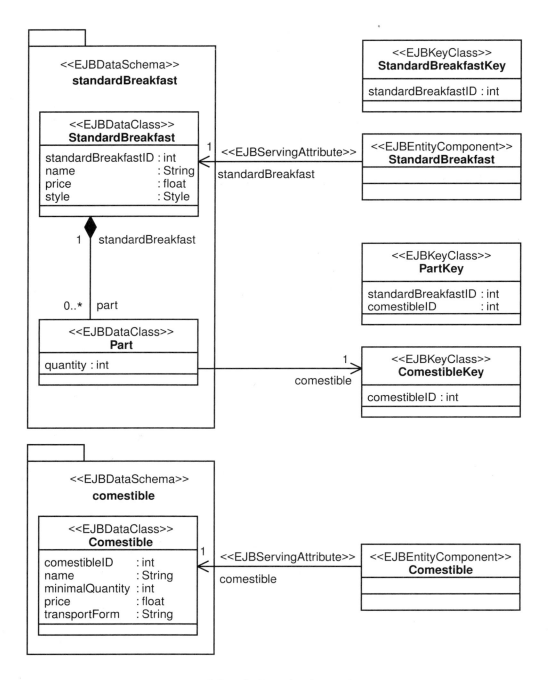

Figure 5-3 *EJB component model including the data schemas*

- The data types in the Web model define user presentation and interaction details.
- In the Web application model there are no key classes; instead, the key classes of the EJB model are referenced.
- Web actions are added that define actions that can be triggered by the end-user.

The Web data schemas define which information is shown that can be altered by the user. One Web data schema is typically presented to the user in more than one HTML page. A user may create, query, alter, and delete objects from the domain. Which changes the user may execute is defined in properties of the elements of the Web data schemas.

5.3.1 The Transformation Rules

The rules for generating the Web application model from the UML model are almost equal to the ones for generating the EJB application model. Again, we will leave out the words *UML* and *Web* whenever the source and target model are clear.

1. Each class that is not part of another class is transformed into a component and a data schema. The component is set to serve the data schema.
2. Each class is transformed into a data class residing in a data schema that is generated from the class that is the outer-most composition of the transformed class.
3. Each association is transformed into an association within a data schema that is generated from the class that is the outer-most composition of the transformed association.
4. Each association class is transformed into two associations and a data class. The associations and the data class are generated within the data schema that is generated from the class that is the outer-most composition of the class that can navigate across the transformed association class.
5. Each attribute of a class is transformed into an attribute of the mapped data class.
6. Each operation is transformed into an operation of the generated Web component that is generated from the class that is the outer-most composition of the class that owns the transformed operation.

Figure 5-4 depicts the Web model generated from the same PIM classes as the EJB model shown in Figure 5-3.

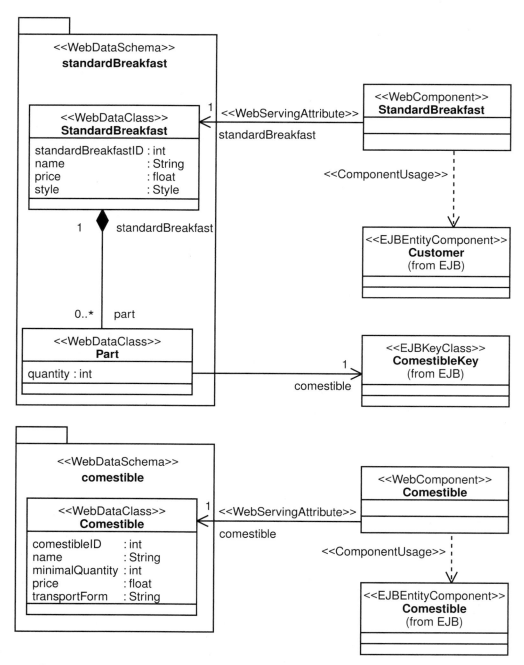

Figure 5-4 *Web component model of Rosa's Breakfast Service*

5.4 THE COMMUNICATION BRIDGES

The MDA process has not been completely described if we do not reference the generation of the communication bridges between the relational model and the EJB model and between the Web model and the EJB model.

In Figure 4-1 on page 46, the communication bridges are shown by arrows. This means that there is a direction in the relation between the two models. The Web model uses (and knows) the EJB model, and the EJB model uses (and knows) the relational model.

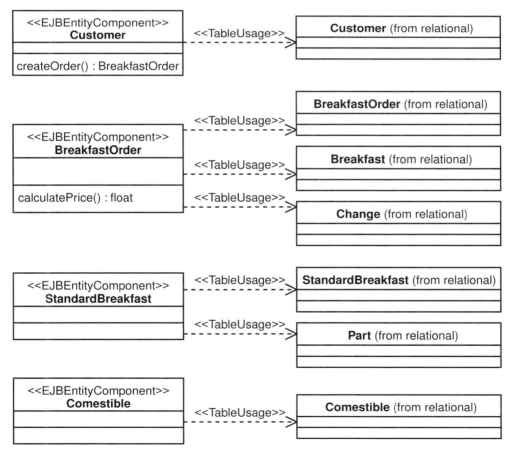

Figure 5-5 *Communication bridge between EJB and relational models*

Both bridges are simple and have been explained. The data storage for the EJB components is provided by a relational database, structured according to the generated relational model in Figure 5-1. The EJB-Relational bridge is constituted by the relation between the table generated for a UML class and the EJB data class that is generated from the same UML class. The relationship between the generated relational model and the generated EJB component is shown in Figure 5-5. The figure depicts the EJB component model for Rosa's Breakfast Service without showing the EJB data schemas, but with all dependencies on the tables of the relational model of Figure 5-1.

The bridge between the Web model and the EJB model is constituted by the links to the EJB key classes and EJB components as shown in Figure 5-4. Note that both communication bridges are relationships between the PSMs. This relationship will need to be preserved when the PSMs are transformed into code.

5.5 SUMMARY

As pointed out earlier, the MDA especially pays off when the transformation process is not trivial, or when the transformation is well-known but involves much work. In the example given in this chapter, both situations are present. The UML-Relational mapping is worthwhile because it speeds up the process. The UML-EJB mapping is clearly a non-trivial mapping, where the transformation rules supply much knowledge of the platform.

In general, we can say that when the structures of the source and target language differ greatly, the transformation becomes more complex. Small changes in the source model may have a huge impact on the structure of the target models and thus on the implementation code.

The process of implementing a PIM is greatly improved by the application of MDA in terms of quality, because we are forced to specify transformation definitions that are generally applicable.

6

Rosa's PSMs to Code

To really implement Rosa's Breakfast Service we have to generate compileable and executable code. This chapter describes the code models and the transformations from the PSMs to the code models. Each of the three PSMs is transformed into a separate code model that is applicable for the specific technology.

6.1 RELATIONAL MODEL TO CODE TRANSFORMATION

The result of the transformation from UML to relational model that is described in this section is a PSM, which is still a model. It is not the code to create the database with. Luckily, the PSM is closely linked to the relational database platform, and uses platform-specific concepts and constructs. From this model, it is easy to generate code.

From the relational model, a pair of SQL scripts is generated. One script is for creating the tables and the other script for dropping the tables. We will examine the creation script only, because the drop script is very simple and does not add much value to the example. The transformation is rather straightforward because the structure and amount of detail of the relational model is already similar to the SQL language. The following rules are used to generate the SQL creation script from the Relation model.

1. For each table, generate a "CREATE TABLE" text, followed by the name of the table, and a "{", then execute rule 2, followed by rule 3, and end with "};".

2. For each column in the table, generate the name of the column, followed by the name of the type, and (optional) size of the column, then generate "NOT" if the column may not have the NULL value and end with "NULL,".

3. Generate a "PRIMARY KEY (" text, followed by a comma-separated list of the names of the columns of the primary key, and end with ")".

Fragments of the generated code can be found in Appendix B.

6.2 EJB Model to Code Transformation

To explain the EJB model to code transformation in detail, we must zoom in on the overall picture of the relations between all models used in the MDA process. Figure 6-1 shows a refinement of Figure 4-1. In it a distinction is made between the EJB PSM that represents the coarse grained component model, as described in section 5.2, and an EJB PSM that is much closer to the generated code. This PSM contains class definitions, and is called the EJB Class PSM. The EJB Class PSM consists of class diagrams where the classes relate one-to-one to the actual classes in the Java code. You

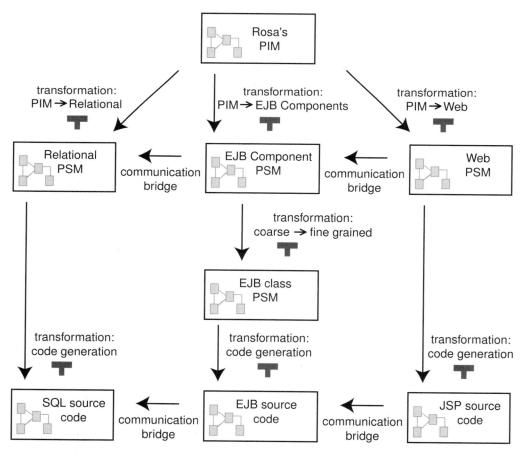

Figure 6-1 *The models in the MDA process in detail*

could say that this model is on the same abstraction level as the EJB source code, but in a diagrammatic presentation.

In this section, we describe the transformation from the EJB Component PSM to the EJB Class PSM. The EJB Class PSM is written in the language defined by another UML variant, the standardized EJB Profile (Java Community Process document JSR26, 2001). Because the generation of code from the EJB Class PSM is very simple, we do not describe it. Fragments of the generated code can be found in Appendix B.

Before explaining the transformation rules, a small introduction to the specific aspects of entity beans in EJB is given.

6.2.1 Some Remarks on EJB Code

According to the EJB specification (Sun Microsystems, Enterprise JavaBeans Specification, Version 2.1, 2002), a person (or persons) who develops entity beans must provide the following:

- Entity bean class and all classes it depends on.
- Key class.
- Entity bean's remote interface and entity bean's remote home interface, if the entity bean provides a remote client view.
- Entity bean's local interface and local home interface, if the entity bean provides a local client view.
- A deployment descriptor written in XML defining some properties of the EJB components. The deployment descriptor describes the transactional behavior of the business methods, and also the persistence strategy for a component.

If an entity bean is managing its own persistence, then in its own implementation it has to call methods of a persistency API like Java Database Connectivity (JDBC). If the entity bean has *container managed persistency,* it does not have to call these methods but only has to set its own attributes. These attributes are copied from and to the database by the EJB container. Note that EJB containers are not developed by the EJB component developer but are completely generic, and work for all EJB compliant components.

For Rosa's Breakfast Service, we generate entity beans with container managed persistency. Besides that, we have to generate remote interfaces, remote home interfaces, the key classes, and the deployment descriptors, which are written in XML.

In addition to the code required by the EJB standard, we have chosen to generate coarse grained components and components that do not need any manually added code to work. This implies that the code model consists of Java packages with classes that implement the data classes in the EJB components. Each data class in Java has

```
┌─────────────────────────────────────────────────────────────────────────┐
│                        <<EJBEntityHomeInterface>>                          │
│                          StandardBreakfastHome                            │
├─────────────────────────────────────────────────────────────────────────┤
│                                                                           │
├─────────────────────────────────────────────────────────────────────────┤
│                        <<EJBCreateMethod>>                                 │
│  +createStandardBreakfast(In breakfast : StandardBreakfastDataObject) : StandardBreakfast │
│                        <<EJBFinderMethod>>                                 │
│  +findByPrimaryKey(In parameter : StandardBreakfastKey) : StandardBreakfast │
│  +findAll() : Collection                                                   │
└─────────────────────────────────────────────────────────────────────────┘
```

```
┌─────────────────────────────────────────────────────────────────────────┐
│                        <<EJBRemoteInterface>>                              │
│                          StandardBreakfast                                │
├─────────────────────────────────────────────────────────────────────────┤
│                                                                           │
├─────────────────────────────────────────────────────────────────────────┤
│                        <<EJBRemoteMethod>>                                 │
│  +setStandardBreakfast(In breakfast : StandardBreakfastDataObject)        │
│  +getStandardBreakfast() : StandardBreakfastDataObject                    │
└─────────────────────────────────────────────────────────────────────────┘
```

```
┌─────────────────────────────────────────────────────────────────────────┐
│                        <<EJBImplementation>>                               │
│                          StandardBreakfastBean                            │
├─────────────────────────────────────────────────────────────────────────┤
│  standardBreakfastID : int                                                │
│  name                : String                                             │
│  price               : float                                              │
│  style               : int                                                │
├─────────────────────────────────────────────────────────────────────────┤
│                        <<EJBRemoteMethod>>                                 │
│  +setStandardBreakfast(In breakfast : StandardBreakfastDataObject)        │
│  +getStandardBreakfast( ) : StandardBreakfastDataObject                   │
│  +ejbCreate(In breakfast : StandardBreakfastDataObject) : StandardBreakfastKey │
│  +ejbRemove()                                                             │
│  +ejbPostCreate(In breakfast : StandardBreakfastDataObject)              │
│  +setEntityContext(In context : EntityContext)                           │
│  +unsetEntityContext()                                                    │
│  +ejbActivate()                                                           │
│  +ejbPassivate()                                                          │
│  +ejbLoad()                                                               │
│  +ejbStore()                                                              │
│  +setStandardBreakfastID(In standardBreakfastID : int)                   │
│  +getStandardBreakfastID() : int                                         │
│  +setName(In name : String)                                              │
│  +getName() : String                                                     │
│  +setPrice(In price : float)                                             │
│  +getPrice() : float                                                     │
│  +setStyle(In style : int)                                               │
│  +getStyle() : int                                                       │
└─────────────────────────────────────────────────────────────────────────┘
```

Figure 6-2 *EJB Home, Remote Interface, and EJB Implementation classes*

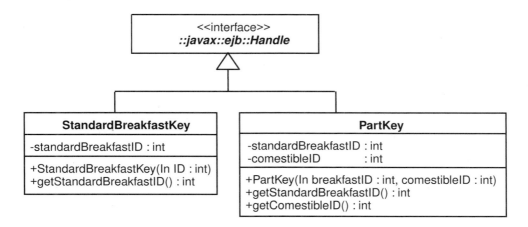

Figure 6-3 *EJB code for key classes*

set- and get-methods and private attributes for maintaining the fine-grain data locally. The EJB component and remote interface need to have methods for getting and setting the data objects remotely. The bodies of the Java methods in the bean implementations consist of procedural code to construct the data objects and process all the changes made in the data objects. Although it helps that we have chosen container-managed persistency, we still have to generate a lot of code.

To make the code of the remote EJB clients simpler, a so-called *data object manager* is created. The data object manager is a normal local java class that creates an instance of the remote interface and is able to retrieve and store sets of data objects.

Figure 6-2 shows the *RemoteInterface,* the *HomeInterface,* and the *EJB implementation* class for the *StandardBreakfast* component. Note that the class derived from the PIM class *Part* does not have its own remote or home interface. It is accessible through the *StandardBreakfast*.

In Figure 6-3 the EJB key classes are shown. In EJB 2.0, the key classes are renamed to Handle classes; therefore, they implement the *javax.ejb.Handle* class.

Finally, Figure 6-4 shows the EJB data classes, which are communicated to clients of the component. As we can see, all access to *Part* objects can be done through the *StandardBreakfastDataObject* class.

6.2.2 The Transformation Rules

It is clear from the above description that generating the code for the EJB Component PSM is far more complex than for the relational model. The EJB coarse grained model abstracts away many details. These details include all the procedural behavior of the EJB components. Because of the complexity of the details, we will not define all the transformation rules in detail, but give a global picture of the transformation rules needed for generating the EJB Class PSM. Because our target is still a visual model, there is no need to explicitly refer to the Java syntax. For example, we will write *"generate a Java class"* instead of *"first generate 'public class' followed by the name of the class."*

The following set of rules is used to generate the classes in the EJB Class PSM for the EJB Entity Components in the EJB Component PSM.

- For each EJB Entity Component, one EJB Entity Home Interface, one EJB Remote Interface, and one EJB Implementation is generated.

- For each business method in an EJB Entity Component, one method in the Remote Interface and one method in the EJB Implementation is generated.

- One "get" method and one "set" method is generated in each EJB Remote Interface and in each EJB Implementation with the corresponding EJB Data Object implementation as result and parameter type.

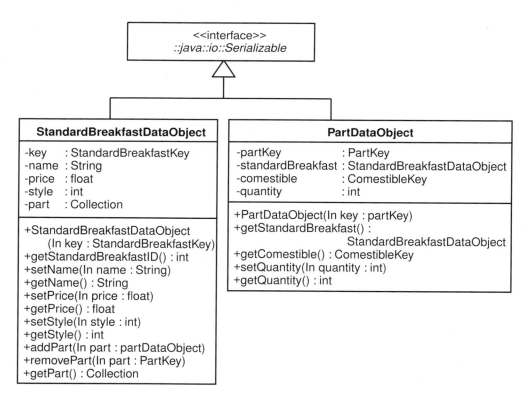

Figure 6-4 *EJB code for data classes*

- All the standard methods (according to the EJB specification) for entity beans are implemented in the EJB Implementation.
- In each EJB Home Interface, three methods are generated: one EJB Create method, one EJB Finder method based on the EJB Key implementation, and one EJB finder method called *findall*.

The result of the method in the EJB Home Interface called *findall* is a Collection that contains a set of instances of Remote Interface that give access to all instances of the corresponding EJB Entity Component.

The following rules are used to generate the classes in the EJB Class PSM for the EJB key classes:

- Each EJB key class is transformed into one Java class that implements *javax.ejb.Handle*.
- For each attribute in an EJB key class, one constructor parameter, and one "get" method is generated in the corresponding implementation.

The following rules are used to generate the EJB Class model PSM for the from EJB Data Classes:

- Each EJB Data Class is transformed into a Java class that implements *java.io.Serializable*.
- For each attribute in an EJB Data Object, one "get" method and one "set" method is generated in the corresponding serializable Java class.
- For each association end navigable from an EJB Data Object with a multiplicity not higher than 1, one "get" method and one "set" method is generated in the corresponding serializable Java class.
- For each association end navigable from an EJB Data Object with a multiplicity higher than 1, one "get" method with return type Collection, one "add" and one "remove" method is generated in the corresponding serializable Java class.
- The types of the Java parameters and method result types in the EJB Data Object implementation for "get" methods and "set" methods correspond with the Java class that is generated for the type in the source model.
- One constructor per EJB Data Object implementation is generated with one parameter with the corresponding Key Class implementation as its type.
- For each EJB data schema, one data object manager is generated with methods to initialize the EJB remote interface and to retrieve and store sets of data objects.

In Appendix B, you can find some fragments of the generated code.

6.3 THE WEB MODEL TO CODE TRANSFORMATION

6.3.1 The Structure of the Web Code

To implement the Web components, we have to generate code that handles user requests from the Internet and that produces HTML as a response. In general, the complexity of this code can be high. A good MDA tool provides its user with transformations that are highly complex, thus creating a fully functional and working application, using well-established coding patterns. In this book, however, we generate Web code with simple functionality using a simple coding pattern. Although this is clearly not a sufficient MDA solution, we avoid long discussions about complex Web coding solutions.

In this example, the Web part of the application is implemented according to the J2EE standard for Web tiers (Sun Microsystems, Java 2 Platform, Enterprise Edition Specification, Version 1.3, 2001). We generate code that generates simple HTML pages that hold query results only. The components are implemented using JSP (Sun Microsystems, JavaServer Pages Specification, Version 1.2, 2001). Each request from a user instantiates one JSP and the resulting HTML is sent back to the browser. We generate exactly one JSP file for each Web component. At run-time, the JSP produces an HTML page containing a table with rows that correspond to all objects of one type (e.g., all customers) and columns corresponding to the attributes of that type (e.g., address and account number).

The JSPs access the data from the EJB components by iterating over a set of EJB Data Objects and getting the values of the attributes provided by them. The iteration is implemented in embedded Java code. The JSP code uses the EJB data object manager for the retrieval of the data objects. JSP supports the access of get methods for the attributes by simply stating the names of the attributes.

6.3.2 The Transformation Rules

The following rules are used to generate the JSP code from Web Components and the Web Data Classes:

- For each Web Component one "query" JSP file is generated with the same name as the Web component.
- Within each query JSP one header is generated containing one name per attribute.
- Within each query JSP one "useBean" element is generated to get access to the remote interface of the corresponding EJB entity bean.

- Within each query JSP one iteration is written in embedded Java using the EJB data object manager to get the collection and iterate over the set of EJB data objects.

- Within each iteration one HTML row is generated with a "getProperty" element for each attribute of the served data class.

- One JSP named "MainMenu" is generated.

- For each Web Component one URL is generated in the Main Menu JSP to access the corresponding query JSP.

- One HTML file is generated that starts up the main menu.

- One property file is generated with the static text on the HTML pages.

- One JSP named "AppError" is generated to display exceptions to the user.

In Appendix B, you can find some fragments of the generated code.

6.4 SUMMARY

In this chapter, we have seen that the transformation of the relational model to code is simple, because the relational model contains structures that can be mapped one to one to the structures used in the SQL language.

To transform the EJB model from section 5.2 to code, we introduced an intermediate model, called the EJB Class PSM. The EJB Class PSM was written in the language defined by another UML variant, the standardized EJB profile (Java Community Process document JSR26, 2001). Because the generation of code from the EJB Class PSM is very simple, we did not describe it.

In order to avoid the complexity that Web code can bring, we have defined a simple transformation from Web model to JSP and HTML code.

7

More on Transformations

This chapter takes a closer look at the anatomy of a transformation. We will see that a transformation needs to be more than the process of generating a target model if we want to be able to maintain consistency between source and target models.

7.1 DESIRED FEATURES OF TRANSFORMATIONS

In section 2.3 we defined a transformation as the generation of a target model from a source model. This means that transformations are purely processes. The process is described by a *transformation definition*, which consists of a number of *transformation rules*, and is executed by a *transformation tool*. In an MDA approach there are a number of features of the transformation process that are very desirable. We name them in order of importance:

1. Tunability, which means that although the general rule has been given in the transformation definition, an application of that rule can be tuned; for example, when transforming a UML String to a VARCHAR in an entity-relationship model, you might want the length of the VARCHAR to differ for each occurrence of a UML String.
2. Traceability, which means that one can trace an element in the target model back to the element(s) in the source model from which it is generated.
3. Incremental consistency, which means that when target-specific information has been added to the target model and it is regenerated, the extra information persists.
4. Bidirectionality, which means that a transformation can be applied not only from source to target, but also back from target to source.

Each of these features puts demands on the transformations. In the next sections, we further investigate the desired features. Section 7.6 describes the implications of the features on transformations.

7.2 CONTROLLING AND TUNING TRANSFORMATIONS

A user of a transformation tool will most likely want to have some control over the transformation process. A response of an experienced software developer to the example in section 5.1 was: "But how do I tell the tool that I want the name of Comestible to be transformed to VARCHAR(20), and the transportForm to VARCHAR(50)?" This developer wants to influence some details of the transformation process, which, in our view, is a legitimate request.

There are several ways in which a user may control the transformation process. In the following sections we describe them all. When choosing your transformation tool, be aware that the options the tool offers to exercise control can be very different from tool to tool.

7.2.1 Manual Control

The most direct control a user can have over a transformation is to be able to manually define which model element is transformed by which transformation rule. This is by definition the most flexible solution, but it is error-prone and much work for the user. Imagine taking these decisions for even a small class model with ten classes, 40 attributes, 12 associations, and 100 operations. You'll be asked to make at least 162 choices. Most users will end up hitting the "OK" button blindly. For larger models, the situation becomes impossible to handle. Therefore, we need to take a look at solutions that scale up in practice.

7.2.2 Conditions on Transformations

Another way of giving the user the power of control is by attaching a condition to each transformation rule. This condition describes when the rule should be applied. A transformation rule will not simply look like: "Every class is transformed into ... ," but something like, "Every class with stereotype <<persistent>> is transformed into ..." In principle, all properties of the model elements in the source model can be used in this condition. Even very detailed rules like, "Every class with string 'THING' in its name is transformed into ... ," or "Every class associated with a class named 'XYZ' is transformed into ... " should be expressible.

Preferably we should make the conditions mutually exclusive. This allows full automation of the transformation process. This approach can be combined with the manual control for those cases where more than one condition holds.

7.2.3 Transformation Parameters

The transformation process can also be tuned by using parameters. Transformation definitions can be parameterized to make them conform to a certain style. For example, when transforming a public attribute to a private attribute with *getter* and *setter* operations the exact prefix strings (usually *get* and *set*) can be defined as parameters of the transformation. When a transformation is performed, the user needs to set these parameters. Providing default values can help to avoid mandatory lengthy parameter lists. Other typical parameters can be the length of fixed-length data types, and so on.

In Rosa's example in section 5.1, the transformation definition from PIM to the Relational PSM transformed each "String" in the PIM into a VARCHAR(40) in the PSM. The choice of the length 40 is rather arbitrary and could better be defined as a parameter of the transformation. This allows the developer to influence selected details that are made during the transformation process.

7.2.4 Additional Information

Sometimes we want to formulate a condition, but find that the information we need is not among the properties of the elements in the source model. As a consequence of this, we cannot write the condition, need user intervention, and have to fall back to manual control.

In Rosa's example, the length of the transformed String in the Relational PSM was chosen to be 40. As we have seen in the previous section, this can better be defined as a parameter. However, it might be not desirable to transform each String in the PIM to the same length in the PSM. The developer might want to use different lenghts for different attributes. A "name" attribute could, for example, have a length of 40, while a typical "description" attribute might need to be much longer (say 256). Whether a String instance is a "name" or a "description" cannot be found in the PIM and needs to be added somewhere.

7.3 TRACEABILITY

In a number of situations, traceability is a helpful asset in the application of MDA. In Chapter 3 we saw that a PIM usually does not contain all information necessary to implement the complete system. A user must fill in the gaps in the PSM manually. When the user has the possibility of changing the PSM, he can potentially also change parts of the PSM that are generated. Obviously, this is a source of trouble.

The least a tool should do is warn its user that the changed part is generated from a PIM. It would be better when the tool can suggest further changes in either PSM or PIM. When, for instance, the user changes the name of an operation in the PSM, the tool might suggest that the corresponding operation in the PIM be renamed as well. An even better tool could perform the renaming. To be able to offer this type of support to its user, the tool needs to trace back the operation in the PSM to an operation in the PIM.

Another situation where traceability is useful is when the project is well underway. The PIM is developed, the PSM is generated and its gaps are filled, code is generated, and then some requirements change. Often it is easier to indicate what part of the PIM is affected by the changed requirements than to tell which part of the code must be adapted. When parts of the code and parts of the PSM can be traced back to elements in the PIM, an impact analysis of the requested changes is far easier to make.

In the case where the system has been delivered and bug reports come in, the parts of the code that are erroneous can be found by looking at the elements of the PIM that represent the faulty functionality. Even when bugs are fixed "quick and dirty" in the code, traceability is an asset, because the necessary changes to the PSM and PIM can be listed by the tool or even automatically executed.

7.4 INCREMENTAL CONSISTENCY

When a target model has been generated, it usually needs some extra work, such as filling in the code of an operation, or fine tuning a user interface for optimal use. When you regenerate the target model (because of changes in the source model), you want the extra work done on the original target model to remain. This is what we call *incremental consistency*.

When a change in a source model takes place, the transformation process knows which elements in the target model need to be changed as well. An incremental transformation process can replace the old elements with the newly generated ones, while keeping the extra information in the target model in place. This means that changes in the source model have minimal impact on the target model.

We can see why minimizing these changes is important in Rosa's Breakfast Service, where one of the target models is a relational model of a database. Rosa might already have a fully populated database in use. If we simply regenerate the complete target model and lose the explicit relationship with the existing target model, we have created a problem. We can create a new database corresponding with the new relational model, but we need to do a migration from all data in the existing database to the new one. If we use the incremental approach, we can keep all the data of unchanged parts of the relational target model without any migration. We only need to migrate the parts whose model has changed.

Note that both traceability and incremental consistency are most relevant as long as the PIM is not a complete description of the system and the transformation tools are not as good as current day compilers. Both are less relevant in the transformation from PSM to code. The implications of these features on PIM to PSM transformations are addressed in section 7.6.

7.5 BIDIRECTIONALITY

The last of the desired features of transformations, bidirectionality, or transformations that can work in both directions, has the lowest priority. Bidirectional transformations can be achieved in two ways:

- Both transformations are performed according to *one* transformation definition.
- *Two* transformation definitions are specified such that they are each other's inverse.

The first way is shown in Figure 7-1. Because of the difference in source and target language, it is very difficult to build a transformation definition that works two ways. An example is where we transform a statechart in a business model to a plain Java programming model. In our transformation, we might transform a state to a boolean typed attribute. It is generally not possible to regenerate the same statechart from a Java code model. There is no way to find from the Java code which attributes should be states in the business model. Even though the two models might be semantically equivalent, the abstractions from the business model are lost in the code model.

In the second way, it is very difficult to be sure that both transformation definitions are each other's inverse. Take, for example, the transformation of public to private attributes from section 2.5.1. We cannot prove that the second set of rules is the inverse of the first set of rules. We simply believe that they are. For more complex transformation definitions, it is more difficult to prove, and our beliefs are tested severely.

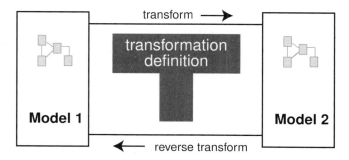

Figure 7-1 *Bidirectional transformation*

As we can see, it is very difficult to define bidirectional transformations. But there is a second reason for giving bidirectionality a low priority. If additional information is added to the target language, or if there is information in the source language that is not mapped to the target, bidirectionality is impossible to achieve. For example, when we transform a business model to a relational model, we only transform the structural information from the source model. All dynamic information in the source model is ignored. It is impossible to regenerate the complete business model from the relational model.

A third reason for giving bidirectionality a low priority is that complete bidirectional transformations between models is only possible if the expressive power of the source and target modeling language is identical. This means that the abstraction levels of both source and target model are equivalent. The fact that a PIM is at a higher abstraction level than a PSM is one of the essential characteristics for getting added value out of the usage of MDA. If bidirectional transformations imply that the source and target models, i.e., the PIM and PSM, are at the same abstraction level, this is not a very productive situation.

In fact, the added value of bidirectional transformations is visible in situations where the MDA process has failed, for example, where a system has been built and the PIM has been lost and must be regenerated. In the following sections bidirectionality is not considered to be a requirement of transformations.

7.6 IMPLICATIONS ON TRANSFORMATIONS

What are the implications of the desired features on the transformations? In short, there are two things we require of a transformation:

- It should have parameters with which you can tune it.
- It should maintain a persistent source-target relationship.

7.6.1 Transformation Parameters

In order to achieve the first requirement, we add parameters to the transformation rules in the transformation definition. For each parameter we can set a default value. For instance, the rule from section 5.1 for transforming Strings to VARCHARs becomes:

- A UML string is mapped onto a SQL VARCHAR (parameter i: Integer [default=20])

Every application of this rule in the transformation process needs to have its own value for parameter i. In most cases the default value will be used, but for the tool to be able to support the requested user control, variation of the default must be possible. The tool might, for instance, produce a list of UML Strings in the source model that are transformed according to the rule above. The user will indicate for which of the UML Strings a different parameter value should be used. In Rosa's example the following table could be shown, in which the user has already changed the value of the parameter for *Comestible.transportForm*.

Table 7-1 *Using Transformation Parameters for the Length of a VARCHAR*

Name of source element	Transformed to	Parameter value
Comestible.name	VARCHAR	20
Comestible.transportForm	VARCHAR	40
StandardBreakfast.name	VARCHAR	20

Of course, the values indicated by the user should persist when the target needs to be regenerated. No user wants to enter those data over and over again. To realize this, there are three options:

1. Add this information to the source model
2. Add it to the target model
3. Create an intermediate transformation object that holds this information

The first option is a popular one; many tools choose to implement transformation parameters this way. The source model, usually the PIM, is augmented with *tags* that hold this type of information. In our view, this additional information clutters the source model. The additional information does not really belong to the source model, it belongs to the transformation. For example, the stereotype <<persistent>> does not really belong in a platform independent model and is just pollution from the business point of view. Using the types *ShortString* and *LongString* in the PIM to solve the VARCHAR length in the Relational PSM also pollutes the PIM. In the case where one PIM is being transformed into a number of PSMs, the PIM becomes overloaded with information that is only relevant to the transformation process.

The second option is popular in lower level tools. For instance, the NetBeans development platform uses this schema to keep information on code that is generated for a visually built user interface. It has some problems though, because a transformation always starts with a source model. Until the first generation has been performed, there is no way to store the needed information. In this option too, the PSM becomes cluttered with information that does not really belong there. Perhaps the best option is option 3. It is much cleaner to store this information as part of the transformation itself, instead of adding it to either PIM or PSM.

7.6.2 Persistent Source-Target Relationship

If we want to ensure that we can keep the source and target models consistent, we have to make sure that no information about the relationship between the source and target model is lost. One way of achieving this is to keep track of the relationships between the elements in the source model and the transformed elements in the target model.

We take a look at how to do this based on the example in section 2.5.2. In this section, the association between *Customer* and *Order* is transformed into two attributes in the classes *Customer* and *Order* in the design model. More precisely, the association-end *orders* is transformed into the attribute *orders : Set* in *Customer* and the association-end *customer* is transformed into the attribute *customer : Customer* in *Order*. Additionally, *getter* and *setter* operations are defined on these attributes.

To keep the information about what has been transformed into what, we can store a link between association-end *orders* in the source model and attribute *orders* in the target model, and likewise for *customer*. This allows us to use the link whenever a change is made in either the source or the target model. The links in the target model

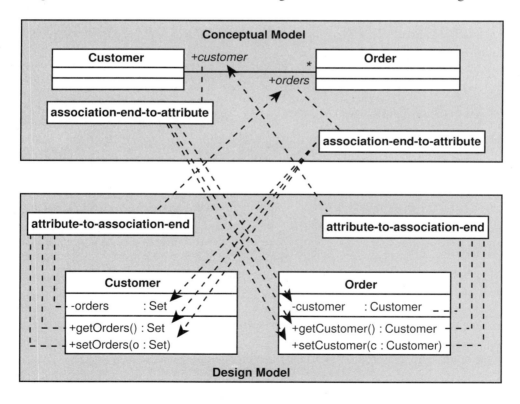

Figure 7-2 *Keeping transformation information in the models*

allow for a transformation back to the source model, while the links in the source model allow for a renewed forward transformation. If we change the attribute name *customer* into *client* in the design model, we could have the reverse transformation to the conceptual model change the role-name *customer* to *client*. Or, if we do not want that change in our conceptual model, every renewed (incremental) generation of the design model could use the name *client* for the attribute instead of *customer*. Without the additional information about the original transformation, this would be impossible.

Keeping these links in the source and target models clutters these models with details that are not really part of the models. Figure 7-2 shows all the additional links that need to be included in the two models. The situation gets even more complicated when there are multiple transformations to multiple target models from one single source model. In the example for Rosa's Breakfast Service in Chapter 4, the PIM is transformed to three different models: the database model, the EJB model, and the Web model. If we follow the approach described above, we need to store all information about all these transformations inside the PIM. It is clear that this leads to large scale pollution in the PIM. The PIM also includes many additional fields to hold the references to the platform specific models. With each new target, new links need to be added to the source model. We need a strict separation of concerns to manage this transformation information in a maintainable way.

7.6.3 Transformation Rules as Objects

The relationship between the source and target model is not a property of either model, but it is really a property of the transformation itself. Using the principle of separation of concerns, this leads us to introduce the transformation as an object in its own right. By promoting the transformation into an object with internal state and structure, we are able to store the required information in the transformation itself without cluttering the source and target models.

For each transformation rule that is performed, a separate instance of a transformation object is created. This transformation instance keeps track of all additional information for the specific transformation rule. Figure 7-3 shows this transformation instance for the Order/Customer example. All links are directed from the transformation instance to the models involved. As we can see in the figure, the models themselves do not contain any transformation specific information. This information is owned by the transformation instance. Also note that a transformation instance consists of multiple objects, each holding a piece of the transformation information.

From the point of view of the transformation objects, the direction of the transformation is irrelevant. Transformation objects contain the information that is the result of the transformation process. Usually there is one transformation object for each application of a transformation rule. In Figure 7-2 and Figure 7-3 the rule *Association-end-attribute* is applied twice, resulting in two transformation objects.

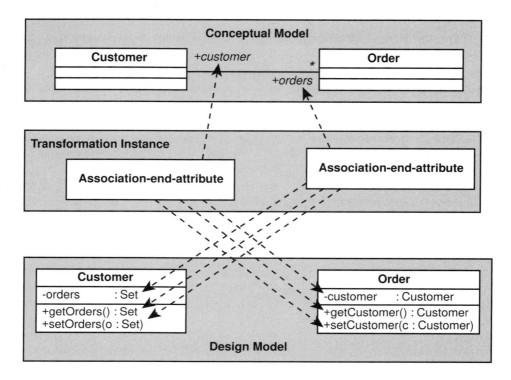

Figure 7-3 *Transformation as a separate object*

7.7 SUMMARY

In this chapter we saw that transformations can be viewed as more than just processes. Because transformations are used in situations where we cannot generate hundred percent complete target models, we need to be able to support changes in both the source and target models. This can only be achieved if we know the relationship between the changing models.

A transformation can be viewed as an instance and thus be able to keep information about transformations between specific models. This allows tools to support changes in both models, while still keeping them consistent. Transformation instances can also hold parameters and/or user choices that were given during the transformation process and make sure that these are stored and reapplied in future transformations as well.

8

Metamodeling

This chapter explains what metamodeling is, and why it is relevant within the context of MDA. The concept of metamodeling is explained using the four modeling layers of the OMG architecture.

8.1 INTRODUCTION TO METAMODELING

In Chapter 2 we defined a model as a description of (part of) a system written in a *well-defined language*. A well-defined language was defined as a language which is suitable for automated interpretation by a computer. The question we will answer in this chapter is: "How do we define such a well-defined language?"

In the past, languages were often defined using a grammar in Backus Naur Form (BNF), which describes what series of tokens is a correct expression in a language. This method is suitable and heavily used for text-based languages, like programming languages. We could use a BNF grammar to define modeling languages. It does fulfill the requirement that it is suitable for automated interpretation. However, BNF restricts us to languages that are purely text based. Because modeling languages do not have to be text based, and often aren't (they can, for example, have a graphical syntax, like UML), we will need a different mechanism for defining languages in the MDA context. This mechanism is called *metamodeling*.

A model defines what elements can exist in a system. If we define the class *Cat* in a model, we can have instances of *Cat*, (like "our neighbor's cat") in the system. A language also defines what elements can exist. It defines the elements that can be used in a model. For example, the UML language defines that we can use the concepts "Class," "State," "package," and so on, in a UML model. Looking at this similarity, we can describe a language by a model: the model of the language describes the elements that can be used in the language.

Every kind of element that a modeler can use in his or her model is defined by the metamodel of the language the modeler uses. In UML you can use classes, attributes,

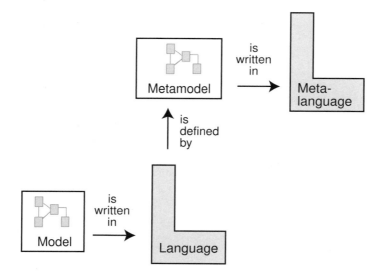

Figure 8-1 *Models, languages, metamodels, and metalanguages*

associations, states, actions, and so on, because in the metamodel of UML there are elements that define what is a class, attribute, association, and so on. If the metaclass *Interface* was not included in the UML metamodel, a modeler could not define an interface in a UML model.

Because a metamodel is also a model, a metamodel itself must be written in a well-defined language. This language is called a metalanguage. So, BNF is a metalanguage. Figure 8-1 shows this approach. But there are few comments that must be made.

First, a metalanguage plays a different role than a modeling language in the MDA framework, because it is a specialized language to describe modeling languages. We therefore use a different symbol for a metalanguage in the MDA framework. Secondly, the metamodel completely defines the language. Therefore, it is not necessary or useful to make the distinction between the language and the metamodel that defines the language; for all practical purposes they are equivalent. Figure 8-2 shows the relationship between a model, its language, and the metalanguage.

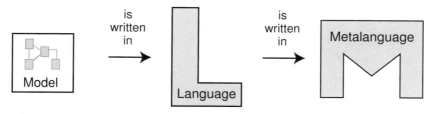

Figure 8-2 *Models, languages, and metalanguages*

Because a metalanguage is a language itself, it can be defined by a metamodel written in another metalanguage. In theory there is an infinite number of layers of model–language–metalanguage relationships. The standards defined by the OMG use four layers, as explained in the next section.

8.2 THE FOUR MODELING LAYERS OF THE OMG

To understand the relationships between the various OMG standards that play a role within the MDA framework, you must be aware of the layers of modeling that are defined. The OMG uses a four-layered architecture for its standards. In OMG terminology these layers are called M0, M1, M2, and M3.

8.2.1 Layer M0: The Instances

At the M0 layer there is the running system in which the actual ("real") instances exist. These instances are, for example, the customer named "Joe Nobody" living at "Universal Road 154" in "London, UK" and the customer named "Mark Everyman" living at "South Avenue 665B" in "Denver, USA." Usually there are many customer instances, all with their own data. These instances may exist in various incarnations, such as data in a database, or as an active object running in a computer.

Note that when you are modeling a business and not software, the instances at the M0 layer are the items in the business itself, for example, the actual people, the invoices, and the products. When you are modeling software, the instances are the software representations of the real world items, for example, the computerized version of the invoices or the orders, the product information, and the personnel data.

8.2.2 Layer M1: The Model of the System

The M1 layer contains models, for example, a UML model of a software system. In the M1 model, for instance, the concept *Customer* is defined, with the properties *name, street,* and *city.*

There is a definite relationship between the M0 and M1 layers. The concepts at the M1 layer are all categorizations or classifications of instances at the M0 layer. Likewise, each element at the M0 layer is always an instance of an element at the M1 layer. The customers named "Joe Nobody" and "Mark Everyman" are instances of the M1 element *Customer.*

M1 elements directly specify what instances in the M0 world look like. The UML Class *Customer* describes what customer instances at the M0 layer look like. Instances that do not adhere to their specification at the M1 layer are not feasible. For instance,

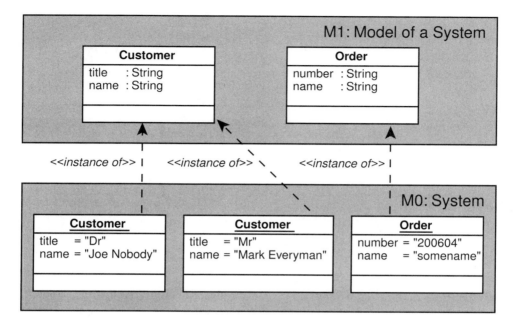

Figure 8-3 *Relationships between layers M0 and M1*

an instance that has a *name* and *city* property, but not a *street* property is not an instance of the *Customer* class, and must be specified by another class.

Figure 8-3 illustrates the M0 and M1 layers with their elements and their relationships.

8.2.3 Layer M2: The Model of the Model

In a modeling tool you can create classes and other model elements. Just like a salesperson creates customer instances and changes them, a modeler creates classes and changes them. From the point of view of the modeler and the modeling tool, the classes and other model elements are the instances they are working with.

The elements that exist at the M1 layer (classes, attributes, and other model elements) are themselves instances of classes at M2, the next higher layer. An element at the M2 layer specifies the elements at the M1 layer. The same relationship that is present between elements of layers M0 and M1, exists between elements of M1 and M2. Every element at M1 is an instance of an M2 element, and every element at M2 categorizes M1 elements. As layer M1 contains the concepts needed to reason about instances at M0, layer M2 contains the concepts needed to reason about concepts from layer M1, for example, a Class, an Association.

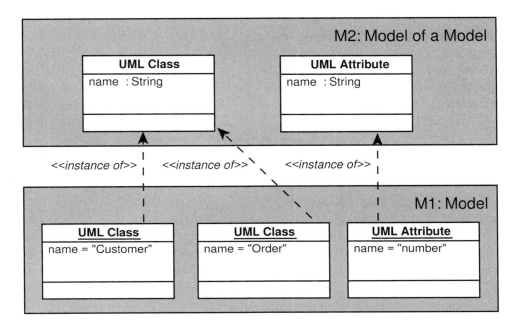

Figure 8-4 *Relationship between layers M1 and M2*

The model that resides at the M2 layer is called a *metamodel*. Every UML model at the M1 layer is an instance of the UML metamodel as defined in UML 1.4 Specification, OMG documents formal/2001-09-67. As explained in section 8.1, when you build a model of a model of a running system, you build a metamodel, a model residing on layer M2, the metamodeling layer. Actually when you build such a metamodel, you are defining a (modeling) language in which to "write" models. UML and CWM (see section 11.7) are examples of such languages.

Figure 8-4 shows the relationship between the M1 and M2 layers. Note that the class *Customer* in our UML model is shown here as an *instance* of the *UML Class* class at the M2 layer. The same *Customer* class is viewed as a *class* in Figure 8-3.

As we see from Figure 8-3 and Figure 8-4, the notation that is used to depict a metamodel is the same notation as used to depict a model. In fact, the concepts used at the M1 and M2 layers are identical. An M1 class defines instances at the M0 layer, an M2 class defines instances at the M1 layer.

8.2.4 Layer M3: The Model of M2

Along the same line, we can view an element at the M2 layer being an instance of an element at yet another higher layer, the M3 or metameta layer. Again, the same relationship that is present between elements of layers M0 and M1, and elements of layers

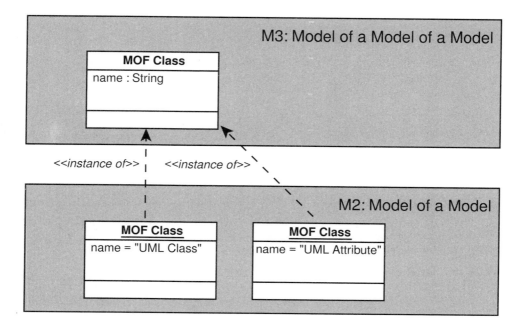

Figure 8-5 *Relationships between layers M2 and M3*

M1 and M2, exists between elements of M2 and M3. Every element at M2 is an instance of an M3 element, and every element at M3 categorizes M2 elements. Layer M3 defines the concepts needed to reason about concepts from layer M2. Figure 8-5 shows the relationship between the M3 and M2 layers. The notation that is used to depict a metametamodel is the same notation as used to depict a metamodel and a model. Figure 8-6 shows the overall architecture.

Within the OMG, the MOF is the standard M3 language. All modeling languages (like UML, CWM, and so on) are instances of the MOF.

8.2.5 Getting Rid of the Layers

In principle we can keep adding more levels, but practice has shown that this is not very useful. Instead of defining an M4 layer, the OMG defined that all elements of layer M3 must be defined as instances of concepts of the M3 layer itself. In fact, the separation between the layers is purely superficial, in order to understand the matter at hand better. What is essential is the *instance-of* relationship. As long as every element has a classifying metaelement through which metadata can be accessed, any model can be build and any system can be described.

Many systems contain their own metadata, which means that the M1 model is physically stored at the same system as the M0 model. Also, advanced modeling tools include the metamodel as well, which means that the M2 layer elements are stored at

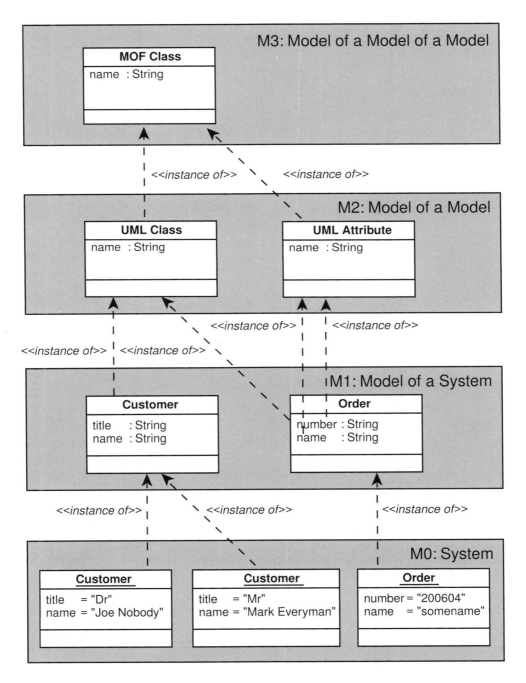

Figure 8-6 *Overview of layers M0 to M3*

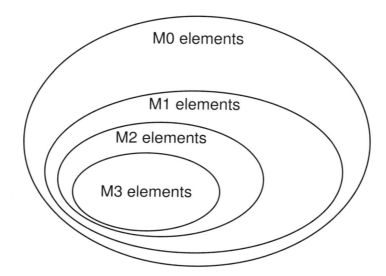

Figure 8-7 *Subset relationships between M0, M1, M2, and M3*

the same system. In these systems instances can have direct access to their types at a higher layer.

Of course, in reality all of the elements from all levels exist in the real world, therefore they all belong to the M0 layer. Some elements at the M0 layer are classifications of other elements and therefore belong to the M1 layer. Other elements at the M0 layer are classifications of the subset of elements in M0 that are the classifications of M0 elements. These belong to the M2 layer. The collection of elements of M3 is a subset of elements of M2, the collection of elements of M2 is a subset of elements of M1, and the collection of elements of M1 is a subset of elements of M0. The Venn diagram in Figure 8-7 illustrates this. The four-layer architecture is simply a structuring mechanism that helps us to reason about models and classifications.

8.3 THE USE OF METAMODELING IN THE MDA

The reason that metamodeling is important within the MDA framework is twofold. First, we need a mechanism to define modeling languages, such that they are unambiguously defined. A transformation tool can then read, write, and understand the models. Within MDA we define languages through metamodels.

Secondly, the transformation rules that constitute a transformation definition describe how a model in a source language can be transformed into a model in a target language. These rules use the metamodels of the source and target languages to define the transformations. This is further explained in section 9.1. For now it suffices to say that to be able to understand and make transformation definitions, we must understand the metamodels of the source and target language.

8.3.1 The Extended MDA Framework

Figure 8-8 shows how the MDA framework is completed with the metamodeling level. The lower half of the figure is identical to the basic MDA framework from Figure 2-7. This is what most developers will see eventually. At the upper half we introduce the metalanguage for defining languages.

Typical developers will see the basis framework only, without the additional meta-level. A smaller group of developers, usually the more experienced ones, will need to

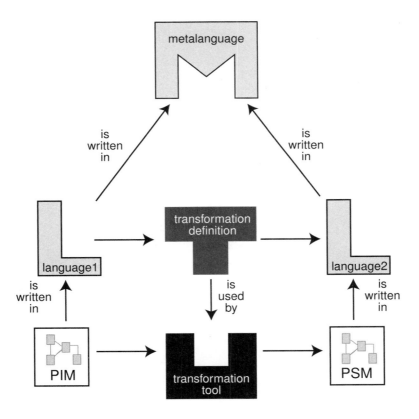

Figure 8-8 *The extended MDA framework, including the metalanguage*

define languages and transformations between languages. For this group a thorough understanding of the metalevel in the extended MDA framework is essential.

8.4 SUMMARY

In this chapter we saw how languages are defined by metamodels written in a metalanguage. The OMG defines a four-layer metalevel hierarchy, although any number of levels could potentially be used. In principle, a metamodel is just a model, but it is used at a different level in the metamodeling hierarchy.

The MDA framework introduced in Chapter 2 is extended with the appropriate metalevels, thus becoming the extended MDA framework.

9

Defining Your Own Transformations

This chapter explains how transformations are defined. Not all users of MDA will define their own transformations; many will be incorporated in the MDA tools. Still, it is good to know how transformations are defined, especially because it enables you to make a more knowledgeable choice of tools.

9.1 Transformations Definitions Revisited

What information do you need to generate a model from another model? You have to relate every element in the source model with one or more elements in the target model. The most direct way of doing this is to relate the metaclass of the element in the source with the metaclass of the element(s) in the target. Because of the instance-type relationship between model element and metaclass, every occurrence of the metaclass in the source will conform to the rules laid down for that metaclass.

Actually, the first transformation rules explained in Chapter 2, The MDA Framework, already used the metalevel, although in an informal way. Here they are again:

- For each class named *className* in the PIM there is a class named *className* in the PSM.

- For each public attribute named *attributeName : Type* of class *className* in the PIM the following attributes and operations are part of class of class *className* in the target model.

  ◆ A private attribute with the same name: *attributeName : Type*

  ◆ A public operation named with the attribute name preceded with "get" and the attribute type as return type: *getAttributeName() : Type*

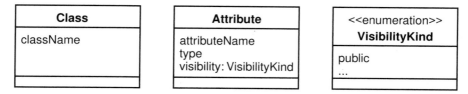

Figure 9-1 *The Class and Attribute metaclasses in the PIM language*

♦ A public operation named with the attribute name preceded with "set" and with the attribute as parameter and no return value: *setAttributeName(att : Type)*

The first rule refers to *Class*, which is an element of both the PIM and the PSM languages. In other words, the metamodel of those modeling languages includes the metaclass *Class*. The first rule also refers to an attribute *className* of the metaclass *Class*.

The second rule refers to a metaclass *Attribute* in the PIM. From the rule we can also infer that *Attribute* has the following (meta)attributes: *attributeName, Type,* and a (meta)attribute that can take the value *public*. We will name the latter attribute *visibility*. The metaclasses *Class* and *Attribute* live at the M2 level as we have seen in Figure 8-4. The metamodel of the PIM language therefore includes the metaclasses as shown in Figure 9-1.

About the metamodel of the PSM language, we deduce that it also contains a metaclass called *Attribute*, as shown in Figure 9-2, with two attributes of its own called

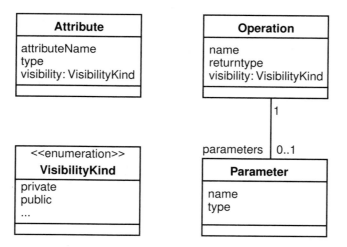

Figure 9-2 *The metaclasses in the PSM language*

attributeName and *type*. This metaclass has an attribute that can have the value *private*. Furthermore, from the second rule we can infer that the PSM language must include a metaclass *Operation,* with attributes *name, parameter, return type,* and *visibility.* The *parameter* has a *name* and a *type* and is therefore a metaclass itself. Because an operation may have a parameter, there must be an association between *Operation* and *Parameter.*

In this example, the PSM and PIM languages are the same (both are UML); we have only one metamodel that we are referring to. Therefore, the enumeration *VisibilityKind* in the PIM language must be the same as the enumeration *VisibilityKind* in the PSM language. The enumeration *VisibilityKind* will have at least two possible values: *public* and *private.*

In practice we never deduce the metamodel of a language from descriptions as we have done above. Instead, the metamodels of the languages are either already available or we develop them separately before writing the transformation rules. This is the approach that we take from now on.

9.2 THE TRANSFORMATION DEFINITION LANGUAGE

In the previous section, we saw transformation rules written in plain English. This is understandable for a human reader, but not for an automated system. In the MDA framework, as shown in Figure 2-7 and Figure 8-8, we need a transformation definition that can be plugged into a transformation tool, which can then automatically execute the transformation. In this section we define a formal notation for writing transformation rules and transformation definitions. Because the rules are not in English but in a formal syntax, they can be interpreted and executed by a transformation tool.

At the time of writing this book, no standard language for writing transformation definitions existed (see section 11.3). Therefore we, the authors, had to define our own transformation definition language. Parts of this language make use of OCL. The purpose of this language is solely to explain the formalization of transformation rules in this book, it is not intended to be a proposal for a standard transformation language. This section explains the transformation definition language used in this book.

9.2.1 Requirements for a Transformation Rule

Any definition of a transformation rule should contain the following information:

- The source language reference.
- The target language reference.

- Optional transformation parameters, for example, constants used in the generation of the target.

- A set of named source language model elements (called S) from the source language metamodel.

- A set of named target language model elements (called T) from the target language metamodel.

- A bidirectional indicator: a boolean that states whether or not a source model may/can be (re)generated from the target.

- The source language condition: an invariant that states the conditions that must hold in the source model for this transformation rule to apply. The invariant may only be expressed on elements from set S.

- The target language condition: an invariant that states the conditions that must hold in the target model for this transformation rule to apply, or that needs to be generated when the target model is not yet present. The invariant may only be expressed on elements from set T.

- A set of mapping rules, where each rule maps some model elements in set S to model elements in set T.

Furthermore, we prefer to name each transformation rule for referential purposes, although this name could be omitted.

9.2.2 A Notation for Transformation Rules

For each of the parts of a transformation rule there is a specific notation. Every transformation rule starts with the keyword *Transformation* and a name. The source and target languages are referenced by the stating both language names between brackets after the transformation name. The first name indicates the source language, the second the target language. In practice the language names would be standard fully qualified names, in the examples we use simple names. The rest of the transformation rule is written between curly brackets. Example:

```
Transformation ClassToTable (UML, SQL) {
...
}
```

The parameters to this transformation rule are written as a list of variable declarations following the keyword *params*. The type of a transformation parameter must be a type defined in either the source or the target language. Example:

```
params
        setterprefix: String = 'set';
        getterprefix: String = 'get';
```

The source and target language model elements are written as variable declarations also following the keywords *source* and *target*, respectively. The type of a model element must be a type defined in the source or the target language metamodel, respectively. Example:

```
target
        c: SQL::Column    ;
        f: SQL::ForeignKey;
```

The directional indicator is given by the keyword *bidirectional* or *unidirectional*. Example:

```
unidirectional;
```

The source and target language condition are written as OCL boolean expressions after the keywords *source condition* and *target condition*. The elements used in the expressions may only come from the source or the target language, respectively and the expressions may only start with elements declared in the source or target elements section respectively. Example:

```
target condition
        f.value = c and c.type = f.refersTo.value.type;
```

All mapping rules come after the keyword *mapping*. In the notation for mapping rules, one new symbol is used: <~>. It is used as an infix operator with two operands. The intuitive meaning of this symbol is: "There is a transformation rule from the source language to the target language that transforms the left-hand side operand to the right-hand side operand." If the transformation rule is bidirectional, the same holds from right to left. Example:

```
mapping
        c.name <~> t.name;
```

The mapping operator may also be used when both operands are sets. In that case its intuitive meaning is: "For all elements in the first operand there is a transformation to an element in the second operand."

For instance, if *classes* is a set of UML classes and *tables* is a set of SQL tables, then the expression *classes* <~> *tables,* means that for all classes in the set *classes,* there is a table in the set *tables* for which there is a transformation that maps that class to that table. To put it more formally:

```
classes->forAll( c | tables->exists( t | c <~> t );
```

When the transformation is defined as bidirectional, it means also that for all tables in the set *tables,* there is a class in the set *classes* for which there is a transformation that maps that table to that class. More formally expressed it means:

```
classes->forAll( c | tables->exists( t | c <~> t ) );
and
tables->forAll( t | classes->exists( c | c <~> t ) )
```

Because all mapping rules conceptually refer to other transformation rules, transformation rules are actually built up in a boot-strapping manner. The base of this boot-strapping is provided by a number of primitive transformation rules, which map primitive data types in the source language to primitive data types in the target language. From this base all transformations can be built using the mapping rules.

There is one restriction to mapping rules and that is that they cannot be defined conditionally. Any conditions on either source or target can be specified in the source and target conditions. As soon as the source and target conditions are true, the mapping rules are applicable.

9.2.3 Transformation Definitions

A set of rules formalized as explained above constitutes a transformation definition. However, sometimes transformation definitions are more conveniently defined by specifying that other transformation definitions are to be executed in sequence. To transform model A into model C, you might want to use the transformation definitions that transform model A into model B, and model B into model C. The reason might be that both transformations already exist, or that they are much easier to define. Therefore, a transformation definition may be defined in two ways.

> *A transformation definition may be defined either by specifying all transformation rules in the set, or by specifying that other transformation definitions are to be executed in sequence.*

In the case of two transformations to be applied in sequence, application of a subtransformation definition results (at least conceptually) in an intermediate model, which is target to the first subtransformation definition, and source to the next.

There are a number of rules that apply to a transformation definition that is defined by a sequence of other transformation definitions:

1. The source language of the combined transformation definition is the source language of the first (sub)transformation definition.

2. The target language of the last (sub)transformation definition is the target language of the combined transformation definition.

3. The source language of any (sub)transformation definition is the target language of the (sub)transformation definition that precedes.

There is in this book no special notation for transformation definitions.

9.3 EXAMPLE TRANSFORMATION DEFINITIONS

This section shows the transformation rules for one simple example. The PIM and PSM languages are fixed. Note that it is easy to change the rules such that the PIM will map to any mainstream object oriented language. The transformation below can easily be adapted to transform to, for example, Python, Java, or C++.

9.3.1 Public and Private Attributes

The second transformation rule explained in section 9.1 specifies a transformation from public attribute to private attribute and getter and setter operations. The rule can be seen as a relationship class between the metaclasses of both PIM and PSM language, as shown in Figure 9-3. To distinguish between the metaclass *Attribute* of the

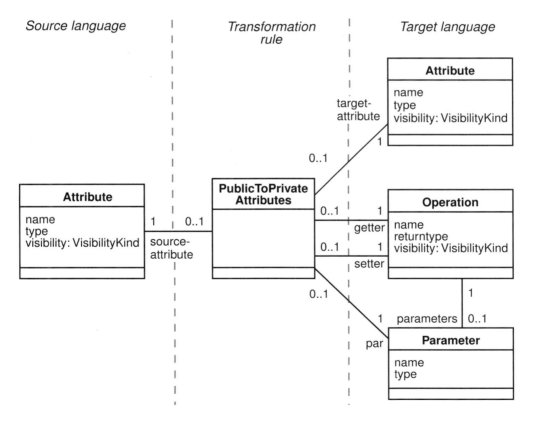

Figure 9-3 *The transformation rule, viewed as a class*

PIM and the PSM language, the role names used in the associations are *sourceAttribute* and *targetAttribute,* respectively. Remember that actually the two *Attribute* classes shown in the figure are one and the same, because both the PIM and PSM languages are UML.

The model specified by the diagram is, however, not yet precise enough to be a complete specification of the transformation rule. We have to augment it with parameters, conditions, and so on. The following specifies the transformation rule completely using the language defined in the previous section. In this case the <~> symbol represents equality, because both source and target language are the same.

```
Transformation PublicToPrivateAttributes (UML, UML) {
    params
         setterprefix: String = 'set';
         getterprefix: String = 'get';
    source
         sourceAttribute : UML::Attribute;
    target
         targetAttribute : UML::Attribute;
         getter          : UML::Operation;
         setter          : UML::Operation;
    source condition
         sourceAttribute.visibility = VisibilityKind::public;
    target condition
         targetAttribute.visibility = VisibilityKind::private    and
         setter.name = setterprefix.concat(targetAttribute.name)  and
         setter.parameters->exists( p |
                               p.name = targetAttribute.name
                               and
                               p.type = targetAttribute.type) and
         setter.type = OclVoid                                    and
         getter.name = getterprefix.concat(targetAttribute.name)  and
         getter.parameters->isEmpty()                             and
         getter.type = targetAttribute.type                       and
         targetAttribute.class = setter.class                     and
         targetAttribute.class = getter.class;
    bidirectional;
    mapping
         sourceAttribute.name <~> targetAttribute.name;
         sourceAttribute.type <~> targetAttribute.type;
}
```

When tools support this transformation rule, some tools could offer the user the possibility to set the *getter* and *setter* prefixes as transformation parameters. Other tools could offer the possibility to choose between using a prefix or a postfix string, or let the user enter the *getter* and *setter* operation names to be used in the generation. Not only can the transformation thus be tailored to the specific needs of the user, tool vendors will still compete in the area of user support, even when transformation rules are standardized.

The complete transformation definition for mapping a model with public attributes to a model with only private attributes consists of more than just the transformation rule *PublicToPrivateAttributes*. To transform a complete UML model, a large number of rules are needed. In this case, all these rules would simply take an element (other than a public attribute) in the source model and produce exactly the same element in the target model and they are therefore not formalized.

9.3.2 Associations

The transformation definition for the second example from Chapter 2 transforms associations to attributes. The association ends become private attributes with *get* and *set* operations. This transformation rule illustrates the fact that different strategies can be used when we define transformation rules. To define the second example from Chapter 2, we can either build one transformation definition that specifies the full transformation, or we can build a transformation definition that transforms association ends into public attributes, and then apply the public to private attributes transformation definition from the previous section to this intermediate model. This approach makes use of an intermediate model and the ability to combine transformation definitions.

Because we have already defined the *PublicToPrivateAttributes* rule, the latter option is the easiest, and we choose to specify the simple transformation from association ends to public attributes. The first step is always to determine the metamodels of the source and target language. For this example, in which both source and target language are UML, we use the metamodel depicted in Figure 9-4. Note that this metamodel is not the exact metamodel from the UML standard; a simplified version is used for this example.

The metamodel specifies that a UML model consists of classes that hold features, which can be either associations ends, attributes, or operations. All features have a type that is a class. For operations, if present, this type represents the return type. Association ends have a multiplicity that is the combination of an upper and a lower bound. A single association is the combination of two association ends. Attributes have a visibility, which has one of the values of the enumeration type *VisibilityKind*, that is, *public*, *private*, or *protected*. Furthermore, included from the OCL metamodel, there is a *Set* that has a class for its *elementType*. Instances of *Set* are sets of objects. Although it is not clear from the diagram, we assume that the type of an attribute may be either a *Class* or a *Set*.

Because we may not define mapping rules conditionally, as explained in section 9.2.2, we have to write two different transformation rules. The first applies when the multiplicity of the association end is at most many; the second applies when the multiplicity is at most one.

```
Transformation ManyAssociationToAttribute (UML, UML) {
    params -- none
    source
        ae  : UML::AssociationEnd;
    target
```

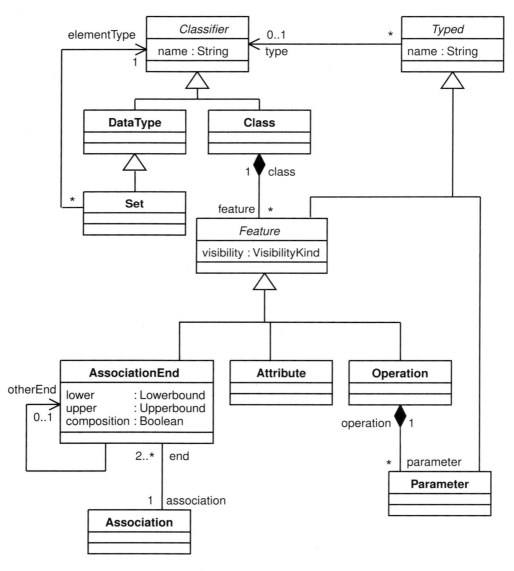

Figure 9-4 *The UML metamodel used in the association transformation*

```
     att : UML::Attribute;
source condition
     ae.upper >= 1;
target condition
     att.visibility = VisibilityKind::public and
     att.type.isTypeOf(Set);
unidirectional;
mapping
     ae.name <~> att.name;
     ae.type <~> att.type.elementType;
}
```

In this transformation rule, the class that is the type of the association end must map onto the element type of the set that is the type of the generated attribute.

In the second transformation rule, the class that is the type of the association end must map onto the type of the generated attribute. Note that type conformance is preserved. Both the type of the association end, and the type of the attribute in the second rule is the metaclass *Class*, as is the type of the element type of the set in the first rule. This is the specification of the second rule.

```
Transformation SimpleAssociationToAttribute (UML, UML) {
    params -- none
    source
         ae   : UML::AssociationEnd;
    target
         att : UML::Attribute;
    source condition
         ae.upper <= 1;
    target condition
         att.visibility = VisibilityKind::public and
         att.type.isTypeOf(Class);
    unidirectional;
    mapping
         ae.name <~> att.name;
         ae.type <~> att.type;
}
```

9.3.3 Classes

Still we have not defined the transformation completely. In Chapter 2 the transformation definitions also state which classes own the attributes and association ends. In the attribute transformation rule, it said:

- For each public attribute named *attributeName : Type* of class *className* in the PIM, the following attributes and operations are part *of class className in the target model.*

In the association transformation rule, it said:

- For each association end there is a private attribute of the same name *in the opposite class*.

We have to state that the generated attribute is owned by the class that is generated for the owner of the association end. What we actually want to define is not a transformation of standalone associations to attributes, or from attributes to getter setter operations. We want to define a transformation of classes to classes, where the association ends and the attributes are mapped as described above, while all other attributes and operations are kept. Therefore, we need the following transformation rule to transform classes to classes. For convenience, we define three additional operations for *Classifier,* called *associationEnds*, *attributes*, and *operations*, which return the classifier's features of type *AssociationEnd*, *Attribute*, and *Operation*, respectively.

```
Transformation ClassToClass (UML, UML) {
    params -- none
    source
        c1: UML::Class;
    target
        c2: UML::Class;
    source condition -- none
    target condition -- none
    unidirectional;
    mapping
        c1.associationEnds() <~> c2.associationEnds();
        c1.attributes()      <~> c2.attributes();
        c1.operations()      <~> c2.operations();
}
```

Here, the meaning of the mapping symbol (<~>) is that there is a mapping from left-hand side to right-hand side, that is, within this transformation definition rules can be found that define this mapping. In defining the transformation for classes, we do not need to explicitly choose the right (sub)rule for transforming association ends. Depending on the way the elements in the actual source model meet the conditions in the transformation definitions, the right transformation is chosen. Likewise, we do not have to bother with the situation where there are no association ends, or attributes, or operations. The mapping rules state that if there is an element that conforms to the conditions it is transformed; if there is no such element, no action is taken.

The additional operations are defined in OCL as follows:

```
context Class def:
    attributes()       = feature->select( isTypeOf(Attribute) );
    operations()       = feature->select( isTypeOf(Operation) );
    associationEnds()  = feature->select( isTypeOf(AssociationEnd) );
```

9.3.4 Finishing the Transformation Definition

The complete transformation definition for mapping associations to public attributes consists of the transformation rules *ManyAssociationToAttribute*, *SimpleAssociation-ToAttribute*, *ClassToClass*, and the rules that map existing attributes to attributes and operations to operations. These last two rules have not been formalized because they are straightforward.

In order to specify the second example from Chapter 2 completely, we have to specify that this transformation is followed by the transformation defined in section 9.3.1, which transforms public to private attributes. The complete transformation definition can be defined as the sequence of the *AssociationToPublicAttributeSpec* transformation followed by the *PublicToPrivateAttributesSpec* transformation, using the names

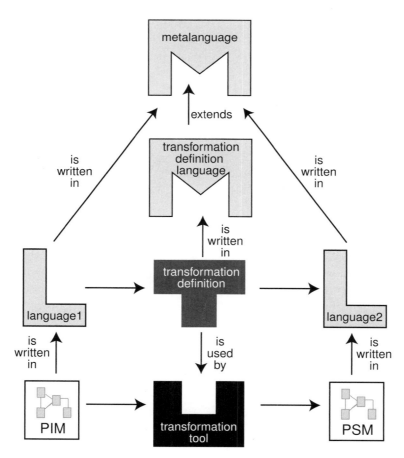

Figure 9-5 *The complete MDA framework*

AssociationToPublicAttributeSpec and *PublicToPrivateAttributesSpec* to indicate the respective transformation definitions.

9.4 THE COMPLETE MDA FRAMEWORK

Of course, transformation definitions need to be written in a well-defined language to allow transformation tools to read and execute the transformations. A language in which these definitions are written is called a *transformation definition language*. In such a language you can define transformations based on the metamodels of the languages. Because it works on the metalevel, a transformation definition language is a metalanguage.

The MDA framework is obviously not complete without a transformation definition language. In Figure 9-5 the complete MDA framework is shown. This is identical to the extended MDA framework introduced in section 8.3.1, with the addition of the transformation definition language.

9.5 SUMMARY

This chapter has shown that transformations can be defined formally using a transformation definition language. To be able to do this, we need to have the metamodels of the source and target languages available.

The transformation definition language, as defined in section 9.2, is not the standard language as it will be defined by the OMG standardization process. At the time of writing, this standardization process is still under way and it seems likely that many different languages will be proposed. It will take some time before this process is finished. The purpose of the transformation definition language in this book is only to explain the formalization of transformation rules.

We have used the transformation definition language to formalize the simple transformations explained in Chapter 2. In the upcoming chapter, the language is used to define some of the example transformations from Chapter 5 and Chapter 6 in a formal manner.

10

Rosa's Transformation Definitions

This chapter shows some examples of transformation definitions. All examples are based on the case from Chapter 4, Rosa's Breakfast Service. The transformations are defined using the transformation definition language defined in section 9.2, The Transformation Definition Language. There is no guarantee that the rules presented in this chapter are 100 percent correct. This is because at the time of writing this book no tools for checking the consistency were available. The intention of this chapter is to illustrate the detail level at which transformations have to be defined in a computational independent manner.

10.1 THE UML TO RELATIONAL MAPPING

This section describes the transformation definition for transforming PIMs in UML to PSMs dependent on SQL. This is the formal definition of the same transformation that has been used in section 5.1 to transform Rosa's PIM into a relational model. In section 5.1, the transformation was described informally in plain English, which isn't likely to allow tool support. The definition in this section, on the other hand, is formal enough to enable tools to automatically perform the transformation.

As we have seen in section 9.2, we need the metamodels of both the source and target languages for a formal transformation definition. In the transformation definition, we refer to elements from those metamodels. We therefore need the UML metamodel and the SQL metamodel. The UML metamodel we use is a simplification of the UML 1.4 standard (OMG documents formal/2001-09-67), and is depicted in Figure 10-1. Note that the example UML metamodel in the previous chapter in Figure 9-4 is an even more simplified version of the UML metamodel. The metamodel in Figure 10-1 adds some generalizations like Classifier and Feature, and adds an AssociationClass.

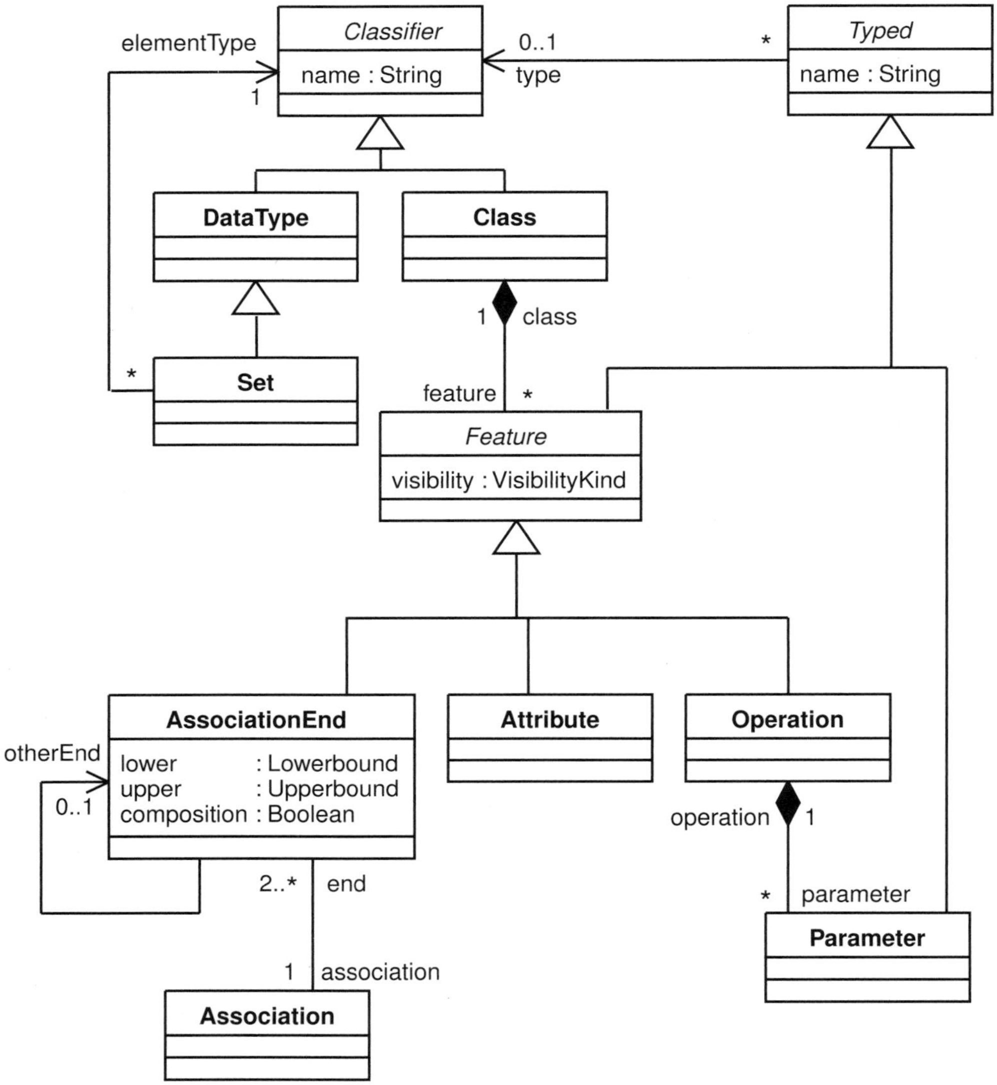

Figure 10-1 *Simplified UML metamodel*

The SQL metamodel is shown in Figure 10-2. This metamodel is a simplified version of the SQL model from the CWM standard (OMG documents formal/2001-10-01 and formal/2001-10-27) and is consistent with the data definition part of SQL (ISO/IEC 9075:1992). Based on the metamodels for the source and target languages, we can now start to specify the transformation definition. In this case, the complete transfor-

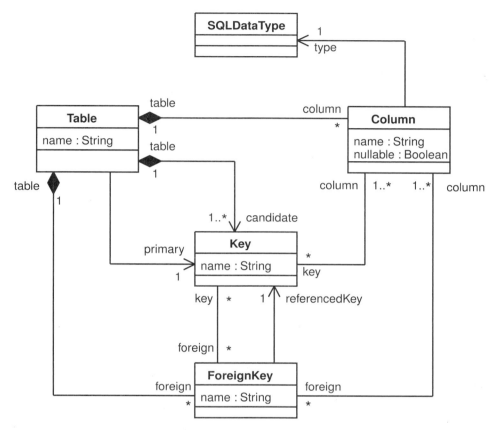

Figure 10-2 *Simplified SQL metamodel*

mation definition has been broken down into two steps. First, we generate an incomplete relational model where the columns of the foreign keys are not fully specified. Next, we take care of the completion, that is, the generation of the columns of the foreign keys.

In the transformation rules, we use the additional operations *attributes( )*, *operations( )*, and *assEnds( )* as defined for Classifier in section 9.3.3.

10.1.1 Transformation Rules for UML to Relational Model

This section describes the transformation rules in the transformation definition language defined in Chapter 9. We will see that the formalization of these transformation rules is not trivial.

1. The first transformation rule defines the transformation from a Class in UML into a Table in SQL. It adds an explicit identifier to the Table, called *id*. As explained in Chapter 9, the mappings in the rule rely on other rules, in this case the rules that will transform attributes to columns and association ends to foreign keys.

```
Transformation ClassToTable (UML, SQL) {
  params
    tidName : String       = "ID"   ;
    tidType : SQLDataType = INTEGER;
  source
    class   : UML::Class;
  target
    table   : SQL::Table ;
    primary : SQL::Key   ;
    tid     : SQL::Column;
  target condition
    table.primary = primary and
    tid.type      = tidType and
    tid.table     = table   and
    tid.key       = primary and
    tid.nullable  = false;
  unidirectional;
  mapping
    class.name + tidName     <~> tid.name;
    class.name               <~> table.name;
    class.attributes()       <~> table.column;
    class.associationEnds() <~> table.foreign;
}
```

2. This transformation rule defines the transformation of an association class in UML to a Table in SQL. The rule refers to other rules that will transform attributes to columns and association ends to foreign keys.

```
Transformation AssociationClassToTable (UML, SQL) {
  source
    assocClass : UML::AssociationClass;
  target
    table      : SQL::Table;
    primary    : SQL::Key   ;
  target condition
    table.primary = primary;
  unidirectional;
  mapping
    assocClass.name               <~> table.name;
    assocClass.attributes()       <~> table.column;
    assocClass.associationEnds() <~> table.foreign;
    assocClass.end                <~> table.foreign;
}
```

3. An association end in UML is transformed into a foreign key in SQL. The condition states that this rule only applies to simple associations, not to association classes.

```
Transformation AssociationEndToForeignKey (UML, SQL) {
  source assocEnd : UML::AssociationEnd;
  target foreign  : SQL::ForeignKey     ;
  source condition
    assocEnd.upper = 1 and
    assocEnd.association.oclIsTypeOf(UML::Association)
  unidirectional;
  mapping
    assocEnd.name <~> foreign.name;
    assocEnd.type <~> foreign.referencedKey;
}
```

4. An association end belonging to an association with an association class in UML is handled differently from a "normal" association-end.

```
Transformation AssociationClassEndToForeigKey (UML, SQL) {
  source assocEnd : UML::AssociationEnd;
  target foreign  : SQL::ForeignKey;
  source condition
    assocEnd.upper <> 1 and
    assocEnd.association.oclIsTypeOf(UML::AssociationClass);
  target condition
    foreign.table.primary.foreign>includes(foreign);
  unidirectional;
  mapping
    assocEnd.name <~> foreign.name;
    assocEnd.type <~> foreign.referencedKey;
}
```

5. An attribute in UML becomes a column in SQL.

```
Transformation AttributeToColumn (UML, SQL) {
  source attr : UML::Attribute;
  target column SQL::Column;
  target condition
    column.nullable = true;
  unidirectional;
  mapping
    attr.name <~> column.name;
    attr.type <~> column.type;
}
```

At the lowest level, we need to transform UML data types to SQL data types. These transformation rules are not defined here, but there should be a number of (predefined) transformations at the lowest level that handle the UML data types to SQL data types. The definition below simply states that there must be such a transformation.

```
Transformation UMLDataTypeToSQLDataType (UML, SQL) {
    source umlDataType : UML::DataType;
    target sqlDataType : SQL::SQLDataType;
    unidirectional;
}
```

10.1.2 Completion of the Relational Model

When the above transformation rules have been applied to a UML model, the result is an incomplete relational model. The following transformation rules take care of the completion, that is, the generation of the columns of the foreign keys. These transformation rules are transforming a relational model into an extended relational model.

The complete transformation definition for transforming a UML model into a complete relational model is defined as a combination of the specification in the previous section and the specification defined by the following rules. The completion rules take the resulting relational model of the rules of the previous section as input and produce a more complete relational model as output.

1. This transformation rule defines the generation of the columns for foreign keys that are not part of the primary key. For each reference from a foreign key to one column in the referenced key, one column is generated that is part of this foreign key. Note that the mapping *"column.table <~> foreign.table"* defines that the table of the source and target of the rule is the same table.

```
Transformation CompleteForeignColumns (SQL, SQL) {
    source
        foreign          : SQL::ForeignKey;
        referencedColumn : SQL::Column;
        key              : SQL::Key;
    target
        column : SQL::Column;
    source condition
        key.table = foreign.table                                 and
        foreign.referencedKey.column->includes(referencedColumn)  and
        not key.foreign->includes(foreign)
    target condition
        column.nullable = false
    unidirectional;
    mapping
        column.name            <~> referencedColumn.name;
        column.table           <~> foreign.table;
        column.type            <~> referencedColumn.type;
        column.foreign->first() <~> foreign;
}
```

2. The last transformation is for generating the columns for foreign keys that are part of the primary key. The tables involved are originally generated based on association classes in the PIM. This rule is the same as above with the exception of a part of the source condition *"key.foreign.contains(foreign)"* and mapping *"column.key <~> key"*.

```
Transformation CompleteKeyColumns (SQL, SQL) {
  source
    foreign : SQL::ForeignKey,
    referencedColumn SQL::Column,
    key SQL::Key
  target
    column : SQL::Column
  source condition
    key.table = foreign.table                                    and
    foreign.referencedKey.column->includes(referencedColumn) and
    key.foreign->includes(foreign);
  target condition
    column.nullable = false;
  unidirectional;
  mapping
    column.name              <~> referencedColumn.name;
    column.table             <~> foreign.table;
    column.type              <~> referencedColumn.type;
    column.key               <~> key;
    column.foreign->first()  <~> foreign;
}
```

Note that in the full transformation definition, rules should be present that map all other elements in the source model, that is, elements that are *not* foreign keys, keys, and columns that match the given source patterns, to exactly the same elements in the target model. These rules are very simple to formalize, and therefore not included in this section.

10.2 THE UML TO EJB MAPPING

This section describes the transformation definition for transforming PIMs in UML to models of EJB components. The definition is identical to the rules used in section 5.2. As explained before, we need the metamodel for both the source and the target language. The source language is UML, for which we already introduced a metamodel in Figure 10-1. The target language is the coarse grained EJB model described in section 5.2.1. The metamodel for the coarse grained EJB components used is depicted in

Figure 10-3. For the sake of simplicity, the transformations and metamodel elements for enumerations and data types without operations (that is, structs) are not defined. These are used for the *Style* and *Address* classes in Rosa's model.

Note that we use some additional queries on the UML metamodel called *getAllContained( )* and *getOuterMostContainer( )*. These queries are defined in OCL in section 10.2.1 as additional operations on the UML metamodel.

1. There is a transformation from each UML class to a key class in the EJB model. For each class in the UML model, a separate key class is generated. This is needed in the EJB platform. This rule formalizes rule 1 in section 5.2.2.

```
Transformation ClassToKeyClass (UML, EJB) {
    source
        class    : UML::Class;
    target
        keyClass : EJB::EJBKeyClass;
        id       : EJB::EJBAttribute;
    target condition
        id.class = keyClass and
        id.type  = Integer;
    unidirectional;
    mapping
        class.name + 'Key' <~> keyClass.name;
        class.name + 'ID'  <~> id.name;
}
```

2. This is a transformation from each UML association class to a key class in the EJB model with two attributes that identify the associated class. Note that this rule only supports association classes between ordinary (non association) classes.

```
Transformation AssociationClassToKeyClass (UML, EJB) {
    source
        associationClass : UML::AssociationClass
    target
        keyClass : EJB::EJBKeyClass;
        id1      : EJB::EJBAttribute;
        id2      : EJB::EJBAttribute;
    target condition
        id1.class = keyClass and
        id1.type  = Integer  and
        id2.class = keyClass and
        id2.type  = Integer;
    unidirectional;
    mapping
        associationClass.name                          <~> keyClass.name;
        associationClass.end->first().type.name + 'ID' <~> id1.name;
```

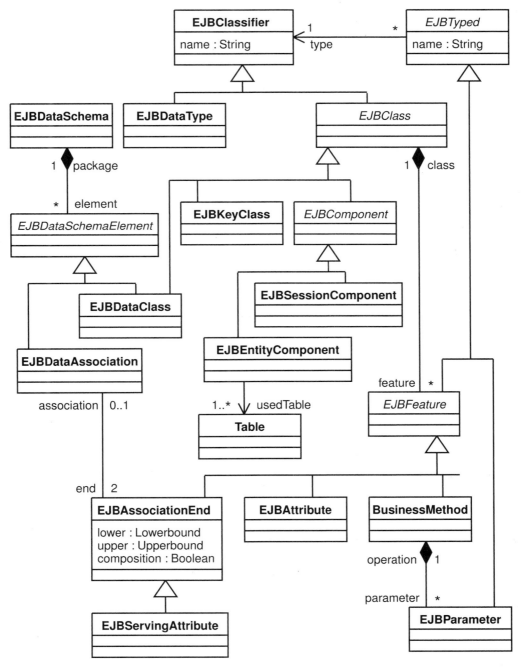

Figure 10-3 *Simplified EJB metamodel*

```
associationClass.end->
                  first().otherEnd.type.name.concat('ID') <~>
                                                    id2.name;
}
```

3. Each class that is not the part of a composite aggregation is mapped to an EJB entity component. Classes that are composite parts of other classes do not conform to this rule and are transformed by the next rule. This rule formalizes rule 2 in section 5.2.2.

```
Transformation ClassToEntityComponent (UML, EJB) {
  source class : UML::Class;
  target
      entityComponent  : EJB::EJBEntityComponent;
      rootDataClass    : EJB::EJBDataClass;
      dataSchema       : EJB::EJBDataSchema;
      servingAttribute : EJB::EJBServingAttribute;
  source condition
      not class.associationEnds()->exists(
                                  otherEnd.composition = true);
  target condition
      servingAttribute.class = entityComponent and
      servingAttribute.type  = rootDataClass    and
      rootDataClass.package  = dataSchema
  unidirectional;
  mapping
    class.name <~> entityComponent.name;
    class.name <~> rootDataClass.name;
    class.name <~> servingAttribute.name;
    class.name <~> dataSchema.name;
    class.getAllContained(Set(UML::Class){}).operations() <~>
                                          entityComponent.feature;
    class.feature->select(oclKindOf(UML::Attribute) or
                        oclKindOf(UML::AssociationEnd)) <~>
                                          rootDataClass.feature;
    class.getAllContained(Set(UML::Class){}) <~>
                                          entityComponent.usedTable;
}
```

4. The following transformation defines the mapping from a UML class to an EJB data class. The source condition states that this transformation can only be applied when the UML class is part of a composite aggregation. This rule formalizes a part of rule 3 in section 5.2.2.

```
Transformation ClassToDataClass (UML, EJB) {
  source class        : UML::Class;
  target nonRootClass : EJB::EJBDataClass;
```

```
source condition
   class.associationEnds()->exists(otherEnd.composition = true);
unidirectional;
mapping
   class.name <~> nonRootClass.name;
   class.feature->select(oclKindOf(UML::Attribute) or
                         oclKindOf(UML::AssociationEnd)) <~>
                                             rootDataClass.feature;
   class.getOuterMostContainer() <-> nonRootClass.package;
}
```

5. Each association is transformed into an EJB association. This rule formalizes rule 4 in section 5.2.2.

```
Transformation AssociationToDataAssociation (UML, EJB) {
   source assoc     : UML::Association;
   target dataAssoc : EJB::EJBDataAssociation;
   source condition
      assoc.end->exists(composition);
   unidirectional;
   mapping
      assoc.name                      <~> dataAssoc.name;
      assoc.end                       <~> dataAssoc.end;
      assoc.getOuterMostContainer() <~> dataAssoc.package;
}
```

6. This rule formalizes a part of rule 5 in section 5.2.2.

```
Transformation AssociationClassToDataClass (UML, EJB) {
   source associationClass : UML::AssociationClass;
   target nonRootClass     : EJB::EJBDataClass;
   source condition
      class.feature->exists(end : AssociationEnd |
                                 end.otherEnd.composition);

   unidirectional;
   mapping
      associationClass.name <~> nonRootClass.name;
      associationClass.feature->select(oclKindOf(UML::Attribute) or
                              oclKindOf(UML::AssociationEnd)) <~>
                                             rootDataClass.feature;
      associationClass.getOuterMostContainer() <~>
                                          nonRootClass.package;
}
```

7. The following rule formalizes rule 6 in section 5.2.2. This is a straightforward transformation from UML attribute to EJB attribute.

```
Transformation UMLAttributeToEJBAttribute (UML, EJB) {
  source umlAttribute : UML::Attribute;
  target ejbAttribute : EJB::EJBAttribute;
  unidirectional;
  mapping
    umlAttribute.name <~> ejbAttribute.name;
    umlAttribute.type <~> ejbAttribute.type;
}
```

8. This rule defines a transformation from a UML association end to an EJB association end. The condition of this rule states that it is only applicable if the transformed association end is not crossing an EJB data schema. In this case, the type of the EJB association end is an EJB data class. This rule formalizes a part of rule 4 in section 5.2.2.

```
Transformation UMLAssociationEndToEJBAssociationEnd(UML, EJB) {
  source umlAssociationEnd : UML::AssociationEnd;
  target ejbAssociationEnd : EJB::EJBAssociationEnd;
  source condition
    umlAssociationEnd.association.oclIsTypeOf(Association) and
    umlAssociationEnd.class.getOuterMostContainer() =
                umlAssociationEnd.type.getOuterMostContainer();
  unidirectional;
  mapping
    umlAssociationEnd.name         <~> ejbAssociationEnd.name;
    umlAssociationEnd.upper        <~> ejbAssociationEnd.upper;
    umlAssociationEnd.lower        <~> ejbAssociationEnd.lower;
    umlAssociationEnd.composition <~>
                                    ejbAssociationEnd.composition;
    umlAssociationEnd.type         <~>
            ejbAssociationEnd.type.oclAsType(EJB::EJBDataClass);
}
```

9. This rule also defines a transformation from a UML association end to an EJB association end. The condition of this rule states that it is only applicable if the transformed association end is crossing an EJB data schema. In this case, the type of the EJB association end is an EJB key class. This rule formalizes a part of rule 4 in section 5.2.2.

```
Transformation UMLAssociationEndToEJBAssociationEnd(UML, EJB) {
  source umlAssociationEnd : UML::AssociationEnd;
  target ejbAssociationEnd : EJB::EJBAssociationEnd;
  source condition
    umlAssociationEnd.association.oclIsTypeOf(Association) and
    not umlAssociationEnd.class.getOuterMostContainer() =
                umlAssociationEnd.type.getOuterMostContainer();
  unidirectional;
```

```
mapping
    umlAssociationEnd.name   <~> ejbAssociationEnd.name;
    umlAssociationEnd.upper <~> ejbAssociationEnd.upper;
    umlAssociationEnd.lower <~> ejbAssociationEnd.lower;
    umlAssociationEnd.composition <~>
                                    ejbAssociationEnd.composition;
    umlAssociationEnd.type   <~>
            ejbAssociationEnd.type.oclAsType(EJB::EJBKeyClass);
}
```

10. The following rule transforms association ends from an association class into associations in the EJB data schemes. This is because we need two associations per association class to implement them in the EJB model that does not support association classes in the metamodel. This rule formalizes a part of rule 5 in section 5.2.2.

```
Transformation UMLAssociationClassEndToEJBAssociation(UML, EJB) {
    source
        umlAssociationEnd  : UML::AssociationEnd;
    target
        ejbAssociation     : EJB::EJBAssociation;
        ejbAssociationEnd1 : EJB::EJBAssociationEnd;
        ejbAssociationEnd2 : EJB::EJBAssociationEnd;
    source condition
        umlAssociationEnd.upper <> 1                            and
        umlAssociationEnd.association.oclIsTypeOf(AssociationClass) and
        umlAssociationEnd.association.getOuterMostContainer() =
                    umlAssociationEnd.type.getOuterMostContainer();
    target condition
        ejbAssociationEnd1.lower = 0                            and
        ejbAssociationEnd1.upper = *                           and
        ejbAssociationEnd2.lower = 1                            and
        ejbAssociationEnd2.upper = 1                            and
        ejbAssociationEnd1.composition = false                 and
        ejbAssociationEnd1.association = ejbAssociation         and
        ejbAssociationEnd2.association = ejbAssociation;
    unidirectional;
    mapping
        umlAssociationEnd.type.name   <~> ejbAssociationEnd2.name;
        umlAssociationEnd.composition <~>
                                    ejbAssociationEnd2.composition;
        umlAssociationEnd.type        <~>
                ejbAssociationEnd2.type.oclAsType(EJB::EJBDataClass);
        umlAssociationEnd.type        <~>
                ejbAssociationEnd1.class.oclAsType(EJB::EJBDataClass);
        umlAssociationEnd.association.name <~>ejbAssociationEnd1.name;
        umlAssociationEnd.association <~>
                ejbAssociationEnd1.type.oclAsType(EJB::EJBDataClass);
```

```
            umlAssociationEnd.association <~>
                    ejbAssociationEnd2.class.oclAsType(EJB::EJBDataClass);
    }
```

11. If we cross different EJB data schemes, we only need an association end pointing
    out of the EJB data schema to an EJB key class. This rule formalizes a part of rule
    5 in section 5.2.2.

```
    Transformation UMLAssociationClassEndToEJBAssociation(UML, EJB) {
        source umlAssociationEnd  : UML::AssociationEnd;
        target ejbAssociationEnd2 : EJB::EJBAssociationEnd;
        source condition
            umlAssociationEnd.upper <> 1                                and
            umlAssociationEnd.association.
                                    oclIsTypeOf(UML::AssociationClass)
            and
            not umlAssociationEnd.association.getOuterMostContainer() =
                        umlAssociationEnd.type.getOuterMostContainer();
        target condition
            ejbAssociationEnd2.lower = 1 and
            ejbAssociationEnd2.upper = 1;
        unidirectional;
        mapping
            umlAssociationEnd.type.name    <~> ejbAssociationEnd2.name;
            umlAssociationEnd.composition <~>
                                    ejbAssociationEnd2.composition;
            umlAssociationEnd.type         <~>
                    ejbAssociationEnd2.type.oclAsType(EJB::EJBKeyClass);
            umlAssociationEnd.association <~>
                    ejbAssociationEnd2.class.oclAsType(EJB::EJBDataClass);
    }
```

12. An Operation in UML becomes a business method in the EJB model. This rule for-
    malizes a part of rule 7 in section 5.2.2.

```
    Transformation UMLOperationToBusinessMethod(UML, EJB) {
        source umlOperation  : UML::Operation;
        target businessMethod : EJB::BusinessMethod;
        unidirectional;
        mapping
            umlOperation.name      <~> businessMethod.name;
            umlOperation.parameter <~> businessMethod.parameter;
    }
```

13. UML Parameters are transformed into EJB Parameters.

```
    Transformation UMLParameterToEJBParameter(UML, EJB) {
        source umlParameter : UML::Parameter;
```

```
   target ejbParameter : EJB::EJBParameter;
   unidirectional;
   mapping
      umlParameter.name <~> ejbParameter.name;
      umlParameter.type <~> ejbParameter.type;
}
```

At the lowest level we need to transform UML datatypes to EJB datatypes. This transformation is not defined here, but there should be a number of (predefined) transformations at the lowest level of UML to EJB datatypes. The definition below simply states that there must be such a transformation from UML to EJB datatypes.

```
Transformation UMLDataTypeToEJBDataType (UML, EJB) {
   source umlDataType : UML::DataType;
   target ejbDataType : EJB::EJBDataType;
   unidirectional;
}
```

10.2.1 Additional Operations

The following query operations are defined on the UML metamodel, and used in the transformations above. The definition uses the OCL 2.0 functionality to define additional operations on existing classes in a model.

1. The operation *getAllContained()* returns a set of all classes that are directly or indirectly composed via a composite association, including the class itself.

```
context Class def:
getAllContained( contained : Set(Class) ) : Set(Class) =
if contained->includes(self) then
  result = contained
else
  let allContained = contained->including(self) in
    result = self.feature->
        select(end : AssociationEnd |end.composition)->
        collect(type)->
        iterate( containedClass : Class ; acc : Set(Class) =
                                            allContained |
        acc->union(containedClass.getAllContained(allContained))
endif
```

2. The operation *getOuterMostContainer* returns the outermost class that incorporates this class through a composition association.

```
context Class def:
getOuterMostContainer() : Class =
if  self.feature->exists(end : AssociationEnd |
```

```
                                           end.otherEnd.composition)
then
  result = self.feature->select(end : AssociationEnd |
  end.otherEnd.composition)->first().type.getOuterMostContainer()
else
  result = class
endif
```

3. The operation *getOuterMostContainer* returns the outermost class that incorporates this association through a composition association.

```
context Association def:
getOuterMostContainer() : Class =
result = self.end->select(end : AssociationEnd |
                                  end.otherEnd.composition)
                        ->first().type.getOuterMostContainer()
```

4. The operation *getOuterMostContainer* returns the outermost class that incorporates this association class through a composition association.

```
context AssociationClass def:
getOuterMostContainer() : Class =
if  self.end->size() = 1              -- is one way navigable
then
  result = self.end->first().class.getOuterMostContainer()
else
  result = self
endif
```

10.3 THE UML TO WEB MAPPING

This section describes the transformation definition for transforming PIMs in UML to models of Web components. The definition is identical to the rules used in section 5.3.1. The source language is the simplified UML, defined in the metamodel in Figure 10-1. The target language is the Web model described in section 5.3. The metamodel for Web components used is depicted in Figure 10-4. The rules depend on the UML to EJB transformation rules. This is because the generated Web components depend on the EJB components, similar to the fact that EJB Entity Components depend on the Tables of the relational model.

As already explained in section 5.3.1. the UML to Web transformation rules are very similar to the UML to EJB transformation rules. This is also the reason why both transformation definitions use the same query operations defined in section 10.2.1.

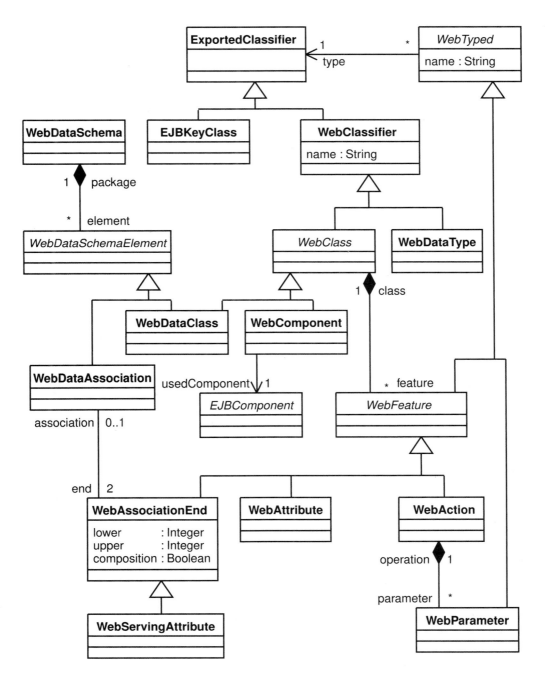

Figure 10-4 *Simplified Web metamodel*

1. Each class that is not the part of a composite aggregation is mapped to a Web component. Classes that are composite parts of other classes do not conform to this rule and are transformed by the next rule. This rule formalizes rule 1 in section 5.3.1.

```
Transformation ClassToWebComponent (UML, Web) {
  source
    class            : UML::Class;
  target
    webComponent     : Web::WebComponent;
    rootDataClass    : Web::WebDataClass;
    dataSchema       : Web::WebDataSchema;
    servingAttribute : Web::WebServingAttribute;
  source condition
    not class.feature->exists(end : UML::AssociationEnd |
                                    end.otherEnd.composition);
  target condition
    servingAttribute.class = webComponent and
    servingAttribute.type  = rootDataClass and
    rootDataClass.package  = dataSchema;
  unidirectional;
  mapping
    class.name <~> webComponent.name;
    class.name <~> rootDataClass.name;
    class.name <~> servingAttribute.name;
    class.name <~> dataSchema.name;
    class.getAllContained(Set(UML::Class){}).operations() <~>
                                      webComponent.feature;
    class.feature->select(oclKindOf(UML::Attribute) or
                    oclKindOf(UML::AssociationEnd)) <~>
                                      rootDataClass.feature;
    class <~> webComponent.usedComponent;
}
```

2. The following transformation defines the mapping from a UML class to a Web data class. The source condition states that this transformation can only be applied when the UML class is part of a composite aggregation. This rule formalizes a part of rule 2 in section 5.3.1.

```
Transformation ClassToDataClass (UML, Web) {
  source class : UML::Class;
  target nonRootClass : Web::WebDataClass;
  source condition
    class.feature->exists(end : AssociationEnd |
                                end.otherEnd.composition);
  unidirectional;
  mapping
    class.name <~> nonRootClass.name;
    class.feature->select(oclKindOf(UML::Attribute) or
```

```
                          oclKindOf(UML::AssociationEnd)) <~>
                                              rootDataClass.feature;
        class.getOuterMostContainer() <-> nonRootClass.package;
    }
```

3. Each association is transformed into a Web association. This rule formalizes rule 3 in section 5.3.1.

```
Transformation AssociationToDataAssociation (UML, Web) {
    source assoc    : UML::Association;
    target dataAssoc : Web::WebDataAssociation;
    source condition
        assoc.end->exists(composition);
    unidirectional;
    mapping
        assoc.name                     <~> dataAssoc.name;
        assoc.end                      <~> dataAssoc.end;
        assoc.getOuterMostContainer() <~> dataAssoc.package;
    }
```

4. This rule formalizes a part of rule 4 in section 5.3.1.

```
Transformation AssociationClassToDataClass (UML, Web) {
    source associationClass : UML::AssociationClass;
    target nonRootClass      : Web::WebDataClass;
    source condition
        class.feature.->exists(end : AssociationEnd |
                                       end.otherEnd.composition);
    unidirectional;
    mapping
        associationClass.name <~> nonRootClass.name;
        associationClass.feature->select(oclKindOf(UML::Attribute) or
                              oclKindOf(UML::AssociationEnd)) <~>
                                              rootDataClass.feature;
        associationClass.getOuterMostContainer() <~>
                                       nonRootClass.package;
    }
```

5. The following rule formalizes rule 5 in section 5.3.1. This is a straightforward transformation from UML attribute to Web attribute.

```
Transformation UMLAttributeToWebAttribute (UML, Web) {
    source umlAttribute : UML::Attribute;
    target webAttribute : Web::WebAttribute;
    unidirectional;
    mapping
        umlAttribute.name <~> webAttribute.name;
        umlAttribute.type <~> webAttribute.type;
    }
```

6. This rule defines a transformation from a UML association end to a Web association end. The condition of this rule states that it is only applicable if the transformed association end is not crossing a Web data schema. In this case, the type of the Web association end is a Web data class. This rule formalizes a part of rule 3 in section 5.3.1.

```
Transformation UMLAssociationEndToWebAssociationEnd(UML, Web) {
    source umlAssociationEnd : UML::AssociationEnd;
    target webAssociationEnd : Web::WebAssociationEnd;
    source condition
        umlAssociationEnd.association.oclIsTypeOf(Association) and
        umlAssociationEnd.class.getOuterMostContainer() =
                    umlAssociationEnd.type.getOuterMostContainer();
    unidirectional;
    mapping
        umlAssociationEnd.name         <~> webAssociationEnd.name;
        umlAssociationEnd.upper        <~> webAssociationEnd.upper;
        umlAssociationEnd.lower        <~> webAssociationEnd.lower;
        umlAssociationEnd.composition <~>
                                    webAssociationEnd.composition;
        umlAssociationEnd.type         <~>
                webAssociationEnd.type.oclAsType(Web::WebDataClass);
}
```

7. This rule also defines a transformation from a UML association end to a Web association end. The condition of this rule states that it is only applicable if the transformed association end is crossing a Web data schema. In this case, the type of the Web association end is an EJB key class. This rule formalizes a part of rule 3 in section 5.3.1.

```
Transformation UMLAssociationEndToWebAssociationEnd(UML, Web) {
    source umlAssociationEnd : UML::AssociationEnd;
    target webAssociationEnd : Web::WebAssociationEnd;
    source condition
        umlAssociationEnd.association.oclIsTypeOf(Association) and
        not umlAssociationEnd.class.getOuterMostContainer() =
                    umlAssociationEnd.type.getOuterMostContainer();
    unidirectional;
    mapping
        umlAssociationEnd.name  <~> webAssociationEnd.name;
        umlAssociationEnd.upper <~> webAssociationEnd.upper;
        umlAssociationEnd.lower <~> webAssociationEnd.lower;
        umlAssociationEnd.composition <~>
                                    webAssociationEnd.composition;
        umlAssociationEnd.type  <~>
                webAssociationEnd.type.oclAsType(EJB::EJBKeyClass);
}
```

8. The following rule transforms association ends from an association class into associations in the Web data schemas. This is because we need two associations per association class to implement them in the Web model, which does not support association classes in the metamodel. This rule formalizes a part of rule 4 in section 5.3.1.

```
Transformation UMLAssociationClassEndToWebAssociation(UML, Web) {
  source
    umlAssociationEnd  : UML::AssociationEnd;
  target
    webAssociation     : Web::WebAssociation;
    webAssociationEnd1 : Web::WebAssociationEnd;
    webAssociationEnd2 : Web::WebAssociationEnd;
  source condition
    umlAssociationEnd.upper <> 1                             and
    umlAssociationEnd.association.oclIsTypeOf(AssociationClass) and
    umlAssociationEnd.association.getOuterMostContainer() =
                    umlAssociationEnd.type.getOuterMostContainer();
  target condition
    webAssociationEnd1.lower = 0 and
    webAssociationEnd1.upper = * and
    webAssociationEnd2.lower = 1 and
    webAssociationEnd2.upper = 1 and
    webAssociationEnd1.composition = false and
    webAssociationEnd1.association = webAssociation and
    webAssociationEnd2.association = webAssociation;
  unidirectional;
  mapping
    umlAssociationEnd.type.name   <~> webAssociationEnd2.name;
    umlAssociationEnd.composition <~>
                                   webAssociationEnd2.composition;
    umlAssociationEnd.type        <~>
            webAssociationEnd2.type.oclAsType(Web::WebDataClass);
    umlAssociationEnd.type        <~>
            webAssociationEnd1.class.oclAsType(Web::WebDataClass);
    umlAssociationEnd.association.name <~>
                                   webAssociationEnd1.name;
    umlAssociationEnd.association <~>
            webAssociationEnd1.type.oclAsType(Web::WebDataClass);
    umlAssociationEnd.association <~>
            webAssociationEnd2.class.oclAsType(Web::WebDataClass);
}
```

9. If we cross different Web data schemas, we only need an association end pointing out of the Web data schema to an EJB key class. This rule formalizes a part of rule 4 in section 5.3.1.

```
Transformation UMLAssociationClassEndToWebAssociation(UML, Web) {
  source umlAssociationEnd   : UML::AssociationEnd;
  target webAssociationEnd2 : Web::WebAssociationEnd;
  source condition
    umlAssociationEnd.upper<>1 and
  umlAssociationEnd.association.oclIsTypeOf(UML::AssociationClass)
    and
    not umlAssociationEnd.association.getOuterMostContainer() =
                    umlAssociationEnd.type.getOuterMostContainer();
  target condition
    webAssociationEnd2.lower = 1 and
    webAssociationEnd2.upper = 1;
  unidirectional;
  mapping
    umlAssociationEnd.type.name    <~> webAssociationEnd2.name;
    umlAssociationEnd.composition <~>
                                      webAssociationEnd2.composition;
    umlAssociationEnd.type         <~>
            webAssociationEnd2.type.oclAsType(EJB::EJBKeyClass);
    umlAssociationEnd.association <~>
          webAssociationEnd2.class.oclAsType(Web::WebDataClass);
}
```

10. An Operation in UML becomes a Web action in the Web model. This rule formalizes a part of rule 6 in section 5.3.1.

```
Transformation UMLOperationToBusinessMethod(UML, Web) {
  source umlOperation   : UML::Operation;
  target webAction : Web::WebAction;
  unidirectional;
  mapping
    umlOperation.name       <~> webAction.name;
    umlOperation.parameter <~> webAction.parameter;
}
```

11. UML Parameters are transformed into Web Parameters. This rule formalizes
another part of rule 6 in section 5.3.1.

```
Transformation UMLParameterToWebParameter(UML, Web) {
  source umlParameter : UML::Parameter;
  target webParameter : Web::WebParameter;
  unidirectional;
  mapping
    umlParameter.name <~> webParameter.name;
    umlParameter.type <~> webParameter.type;
}
```

Analogous to the UML to EJB transformation, we need to transform UML data types to Web data types. This transformation is not defined here, but there should be a number of (predefined) transformations at the lowest level of UML to Web data types. The definition below simply states that there must be such a transformation from UML to Web data types.

```
Transformation UMLDataTypeToWebDataType (UML, Web) {
    source umlDataType : UML::DataType;
    target webDataType : Web::WebDataType;
    unidirectional;
}
```

10.4 SUMMARY

This chapter has shown the formal definitions of the transformations for Rosa's system. The formal definition is quite long and far from trivial; every detail needs to be correct. It is a time-consuming task to write it, and a good tool for checking the consistency is required. However, we must realize that without applying MDA, these kinds of transformations have always been executed by hand and not automated nor well defined. After the formalization is completed, it can be used many times in many projects and the payback can be huge.

OMG Standards and Additional Technologies

This chapter explains the various OMG standards that are relevant within the context of MDA.

11.1 INTRODUCTION

The concepts underpinning MDA can be applied without the use of standards. However, to enable productive use of MDA it is necessary to have a set of related standards on modeling. This allows the industry to develop tools and enables interoperability of MDA solutions and tools.

Some of the most important modeling standards are defined by the OMG. In this chapter we describe the relevant standards with a special focus on the way they fit together. Figure 11-1 gives examples of some elements of the MDA framework that have been defined by the OMG. Figure 11-2 gives some examples of elements that fit the MDA, although they have not been defined by the OMG.

11.2 THE MOF

The MOF (OMG document number formal/2002-04-03) is an OMG standard that defines the language to define modeling languages. The MOF resides in the M3 layer, as explained in Figure 8-6. As there is no higher layer, the MOF is defined using the MOF itself. It is the language in which the UML and CWM (see section 11.7) definitions, that is, the UML and CWM metamodels, are written. A simplified version of the MOF model is shown in Figure 11-3.

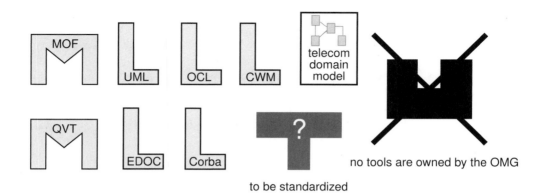

Figure 11-1 *Some MDA elements owned by the OMG*

11.2.1 yMOF Tools

The MOF is not only used to define modeling languages, but also to enable the building of tools for defining modeling languages. The MOF therefore provides some additional functionality.

The MOF Repository Interface

The MOF definition includes a specification of the interface for a MOF repository. This interface allows us to get information about M1 models from a MOF-based repository. This interface is defined using CORBA-IDL and is therefore usable in many environments. Especially for Java, there is a native interface providing the same

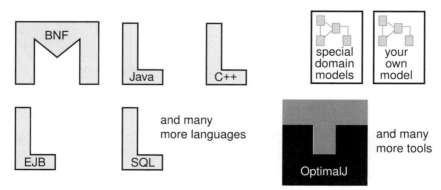

Figure 11-2 *Non-OMG elements that fit in the MDA framework*

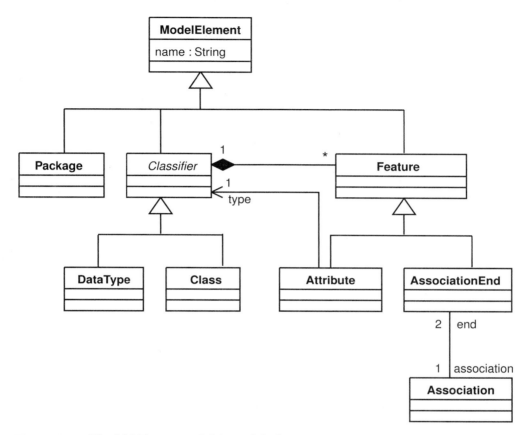

Figure 11-3 *The MOF metamodel (simplified)*

functionality. This is called the Java Metadata Interface (JMI) and it is described in Sun Microsystems, *Java Metadata Interface Specification, Version 1.0* (2002). From Java applications, this interface is easier to use than the CORBA-to-Java mapping.

Model Interchange

The MOF is also used to define a stream- or file-based interchange format for M1 models. Whenever a modeling language is defined using a metamodel described in the MOF, the MOF defines a standard way to generate an interchange format for models in that language. This interchange format is based on XML, and it is called XMI (XML Metadata Interchange). Because the MOF is defined using itself, XMI can be used to generate standard interchange formats for metamodels as well.

The main usage of XMI has been as an interchange format of UML models, which has led people to view XMI as the UML interchange format. Although this is undoubtedly true, this is only a limited view of XMI.

11.2.2 The Role of the MOF in MDA

The role of the MOF within MDA is that it gives us the concepts and tools to reason about modeling languages. Using the MOF definition of a modeling language (that is, the metamodel on layer M2) we can define transformations between modeling languages. Because transformations are defined in terms of the metamodels of the involved modeling language, they can be applied to any model (at the M1 layer) written in one of those languages. Without a standard language to describe metamodels, transformations could not be defined properly and the MDA approach would be very difficult to realize. As such, the MOF is the core enabling technology for MDA.

11.3 QUERY, VIEWS, AND TRANSFORMATIONS

Currently a new standard is under development, called the Query, Views, and Transformations Standard (QVT). This standard addresses the way transformations are achieved between models whose languages are defined using the MOF. It will become part of the MOF, and will have the following parts:

- A language for creating views on model
- A language for querying model
- A language for writing transformation definitions

The latter part is the one that is the most relevant to MDA. It will in time be a standardized replacement of the transformation definition language we have defined in section 9.2.

11.4 UML

UML (OMG documents formal/2001-09-67) is the standard modeling language at the M2 level, defined using the MOF. A vast majority of the models that are being developed are UML models. To be able to use MDA in software development, it is therefore necessary to understand UML.

11.4.1 The UML Metamodel

UML is the most widely used modeling language defined in the MOF. Figure 11-4 shows an extension of the UML metamodel used in Chapter 9 and Chapter 10. It is still a small and simplified part of the standard metamodel, describing only part of the language. The UML metamodel describes *exactly* how a UML model is structured. From the metamodel, we can deduce the following:

- At the top we see that everything in UML is a ModelElement and has a "name."
- The abstract metaclass Classifier is a generalization of Class, Interface, and DataType. They have much in common, but some specifics as well.
- A Class may implement an Interface, but a DataType or an Interface may not.
- A Feature (Attribute, AssociationEnd or Operation) is part of exactly one Classifier; it can never be part of multiple Classifiers.
- An association has a minimum of two association-ends, but may have more.
- An operation may have zero or more parameters.

Any UML model must fulfill these rules; otherwise, it is not a proper instance of the UML metamodel. Because of this, we can reason about UML models knowing exactly what they look like and how they are structured.

Relationship between UML and the MOF

The UML metamodel is an instance of the MOF model. In Figure 8-5 in Chapter 8, a small part of the UML metamodel is shown as an instance model, with each class in the UML metamodel being an instance of a MOF class. More commonly, the UML metamodel is shown as a model itself, as in Figure 11-4.

Additionally, the UML metamodel has the same structure as the MOF model, reusing part of its definition. Because UML is used to model much more than metamodels only, it contains many more metaclasses than the MOF. Examples of this are the metaclasses needed for statecharts, interactions, and so on, in UML.

11.4.2 The Role of UML in MDA

There are two different ways in which UML can be applied in MDA. First, a developer must be able to use UML to create a model of the system that will be built. He should know how and where to apply the UML language to develop models that are precise and consistent enough to be used within MDA. There are many books available that give information on how to use UML for this purpose.

A special and much smaller group of developers will have the task to define transformations between models. This group does not develop a model of a particular system, but instead defines transformations to be used for many models, models of many

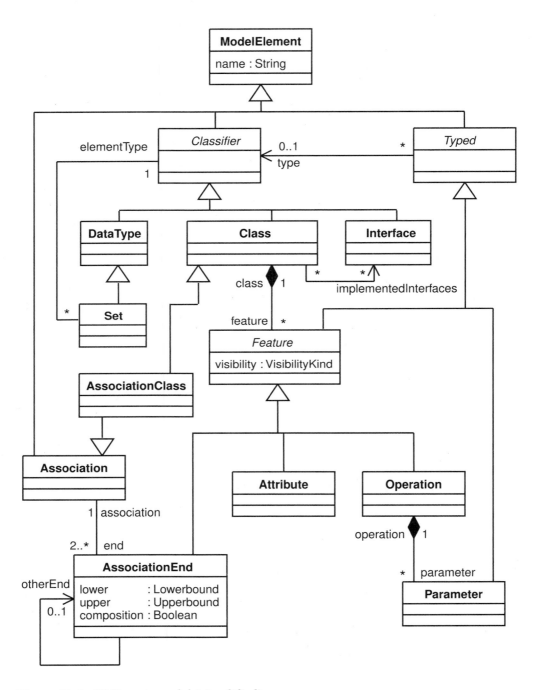

Figure 11-4 *UML metamodel (simplified)*

different systems. We will call these people metadevelopers. Like a developer, a meta-developer must have a thorough understanding of the UML language and its usage. Additionally, he needs to be intimately familiar with the UML metamodel. It is in terms of this metamodel that he or she will need to define the MDA transformations.

11.5 OCL

OCL (OMG document ad/02-05-09, 2002) is an expression language in which you can write expressions over models, for instance, derivation rules for attributes, the body of query operations, invariants, and pre- and postconditions. OCL can be used for both MOF and UML models. Using OCL extends the expressive power of UML/MOF, and allows the modeler to create more precise and more extensive models.

Any OCL expression evaluates to a value. OCL is a specification language and an OCL expression always describes *what* the value is, but never dictates *how* the expression should be calculated. Of course, OCL expressions can be translated to programming languages (for example, Java) to specify how the expression is executed. OCL expressions are "pure" expressions in the sense that they never have side effects.

11.5.1 Using OCL with UML

Traditionally, OCL has been used in UML to specify constraints. The most common types of constraints are invariants, preconditions, and postconditions. More recently the use of OCL for other types of expressions has become popular. This includes the use of OCL for the following purposes:

- Specifying initial attribute values
- Specifying the derivation rules for attributes or associations
- Specifying the body of query operations
- Specifying the targets for messages being sent
- Specifying guard conditions in statecharts
- Specifying end-user queries on a UML model

A UML model of a system becomes more precise and more complete by applying OCL. In the context of MDA, this means that the source model of a transformation becomes much richer, which makes it possible to generate a much more complete target model. The ability to specify a precise and complete source model allows an MDA transformation to generate more of the PSM or code. The value of the MDA approach to the developers is enhanced considerably. OCL is used for specifying expressions in

UML models by any developer that uses UML. As such, all developers can benefit from the added precision and expressiveness.

11.5.2 Using OCL with the MOF

As explained above, OCL can be used at the MOF layer as well, allowing one to write expressions over metamodels. The first usage of OCL with the MOF has been in the definition of the UML metamodel. Several hundreds of invariants, or so-called "well-formedness rules," were written in OCL to complete the diagrams that depict the metamodel graphically. The same approach is taken in the definition of other OMG standards, such as CWM and the MOF itself.

This results in the same advantages as the use of OCL gives to UML models. The metamodels become more precise and constitute a better specification with less ambiguity. For the definition of standards this is even more important than for other models.

11.5.3 The Role of OCL in MDA

In addition to bringing more precision to source models and to language definitions, OCL can be used very effectively in the definition of transformations, as the transformation definition language described in section 9.2 shows. A transformation maps one or more elements in a source model to one or more elements in a target model. One OCL query specifies the elements in the source model of a transformation, while a second OCL expression specifies the elements in the target model.

Many transformations can only be applied under certain conditions. These conditions can be specified in OCL too, one OCL condition on the source elements to be mapped, a second OCL condition on the target elements. All OCL expressions used in a transformation definition are specified on the metamodel of the source and target languages.

11.6 The UML Action Semantics

The UML Action Semantics, as described in OMG document ptc/2002-01-09, is an extension of UML providing the metamodel for a so-called action language. The purpose of this action language is to provide a foundation for dynamic semantics of UML. In principle, the action semantics can be used to write directly executable UML models (see also section 3.2.2) as is shown in Mellor and Balcer 2002 and in Kennedy Carter White Paper, CTN 80, v2.2.

There is no concrete syntax for the action semantics given in the standard; therefore, you cannot write any statement in the language in a standardized way. There are several vendor-specific languages that claim to map to the abstract syntax of the action semantics. The Action Semantics attaches all dynamics of a system to statemachines and is mainly used in the domain of embedded software.

The concepts in the Action Semantics are defined at a very low level. For instance, the concepts input and output pin are defined, which represent the fact that an action (function/operation) may have input and/or output parameters. In many respects the action semantics looks more like UML assembler than a language that is useful for a UML modeler. As such, it might be useful as a foundation, but leaves a definite need for a language at a higher level of abstraction.

11.7 CWM

CWM, as described in OMG documents formal/2001-10-01 and formal/2001-10-270, is a modeling language that is specifically meant to model data warehousing applications. The metamodel has a lot in common with the UML metamodel, but it has a number of special metaclasses, for example, for modeling relational databases. The developers of CWM have removed everything from UML that was not needed for their purpose, and added the specific data warehousing details. The behavioral parts of the UML metamodel (like statemachines or collaborations) are not in CWM.

Because data warehousing is a technology that combines information from many different sources, the CWM metamodel includes simple metamodels for a number of things:

- Relational databases
- Records or structures
- OLAP
- XML
- Transformations (not as in MDA!)
- Visualization of information
- Data Mining
- Multidimensional databases
- Business metadata
- Warehouse processes
- Warehouse operation

As can be seen from the (partial) list above, CWM has a very broad scope. Most of the individual metamodels for the various areas are targeted towards warehousing applications and cannot be used in more general applications without additions and/or changes.

The CWM metamodel(s) are all modeled using the MOF. Therefore, they can all be used as source or target for MDA transformations.

11.8 UML Profiles

The profile concept is a specialization mechanism defined as part of UML. A profile defines a specific way of using UML. For example, the CORBA Profile for UML defines a specific way of using UML to model CORBA interfaces, and the Java Profile for UML defines a way to model Java source code in UML.

A *profile* is defined by a set of stereotypes, a set of related constraints, and a set of tagged values.

A *stereotype* definition has a name and is attached to elements in the UML metamodel. For example, the stereotype <<JavaClass>> is defined for the UML metaclass Class (see Figure 11-4) in the EJB Profile (Sun Microsystems, Enterprise JavaBeans Specification, Version 2.1, 2002). In a UML model one can apply this stereotype to each class in a model.

A *constraint* can be attached to a stereotype definition. This constraint is expressed in OCL in terms of the UML metamodel, and describes the restrictions on instances of the model elements to which the stereotype is applied. For example, for each class in a UML model labeled with the stereotype <<JavaClass>>, the following constraint should hold: "A Java class may have at most one superclass."

A *tagged value* is an additional meta-attribute that is attached to a UML metaclass in the UML metamodel. A tagged value has a name and a type and is attached to a specific stereotype. It can be given a value in a model, but only for elements that have the corresponding stereotype.

The effect of a profile is that it defines a specialized variant of UML, for a specific purpose. An alternative is to define a new metamodel instead of using a profile. This would result in separate metamodels for Java, CORBA, and so on.

11.8.1 The Role of Profiles in MDA

A profile defines a specialized metamodel, which is by definition a subset of the UML metamodel. In fact, a profile defines a new language by reusing the UML metamodel.

Most profiles that are currently used define languages specific for certain platforms, like CORBA, Java, or C++ profiles. A model with such a profile and its applied stereotypes can only be used as a PSM.

11.9 Summary

There are many, many standards that may have a relationship with MDA. The most important one is the MOF standard that allows us to define metamodels. In addition to the MOF, we need a transformation definition language to describe transformations between models. In the transformation definition language we may also use OCL to specify queries and conditions. Although there is no transformation language standardized yet, it is expected to have similar features to the one defined in section 9.2.

All the other languages and standards that we have seen only play the role of source and/or target language within MDA. Furthermore, whenever we define a new language through a MOF metamodel, it can be used within an MDA environment. The UML language and all of its derivatives defined by profiles are the modeling languages that will be used often, but are not essential to the MDA approach.

12

The MDA Promise

This chapter describes future developments that are triggered by the MDA. It describes what is not yet realized, but what is achievable if we follow in the direction the MDA is going. Some of these developments may take place within a couple of years, others might take longer.

12.1 THE MDA PARADIGM SHIFT

In Chapter 1 we explained that the MDA development life cycle is not very different from the traditional life cycle. What is crucial is that the MDA, when fully implemented, will establish a shift of focus within the life cycle. To explain this vision on the MDA we will take a look at the history of programming.

12.1.1 A Historic Perspective

In short, we can characterize the history of programming along the time line given in Table 12-1. Each period is characterized by the dominant type of programming language. The programming languages used in each period are built on the assets of the previous period.

First there was raw machine code, which automated the wiring of computers. Next, symbolic representations of this raw machine language, called assembly languages, were made, and assembly language programs were converted to machine code by an automated tool called an assembler. Following, there was the time of the procedural programming languages. These were built on top of assembly languages. They were designed to be easier than an assembly language for a human to understand, including things like named variables, procedures, subroutines, and so on. Compilers or interpreters were used to convert the programs into assembly or raw machine code.

Object-oriented programming languages were built on the assets of procedural languages. They extend the procedural languages with much more powerful structuring

Table 12-1 *History of Programming*

Years	Programming was done by...
1950	Raw machine code
1950–1965	Assembly languages
1965–1985	Procedural programming languages
1985–today	Object-oriented programming languages
today– . . .	What is next?

mechanisms. Often compilers for object-oriented programming languages use a two-step method. First the program is translated into a low-level third-generation language, next this result is compiled into machine code.

12.1.2 A Shift of Focus

Looking back, we see that there has been a shift of focus in the development of computer programs over the years. In the early years the focus was on writing programs using low-level constructs. Later the focus shifted to writing programs using higher level constructs. The fact that these higher level programs had to be translated to programs using lower level constructs is almost forgotten. Programmers need not worry about generating assembly or raw machine code, because the task has been automated and one can rely on a compiler.

Taking the MDA approach, the focus will shift to another level. Nowadays the focus is on code, often written in an object-oriented programming language. In the future the focus will shift to writing the PSM, and from there to writing the PIM. People will forget the fact that the PSM needs to be transformed into code because generating the code will be automated. Maybe some years later there will even be people who will forget that a PIM needs to be transformed into a PSM.

In the future the MDA development life cycle will not be shown to include an artifact called *code* as we did in Figure 1-2 in Chapter 1. Instead, it will look more like Figure 12-1, leaving out the gray parts. Most people will think that when the PSM is completed, one can go directly to the testing phase.

12.1.3 Too Good to Be True?

When explaining the MDA to software developers, we often get a sceptical response. A typical reply is, "This can never work. You cannot generate a complete working program from a model. You will always need to adjust the code." Is the MDA really too good to be true?

Well, we don't think so; otherwise, we would not have bothered writing this book. We believe that the MDA will change the future of software development radically. One argument for this is that although the MDA is still in its infancy, you can today achieve great gains in productivity, portability, interoperability, and maintenance effort by applying the MDA using a good transformation tool. Therefore it is, and will be, used even when not all of the elements of the framework have been established yet, like the transformation definition language. A second argument comes from the history of computing.

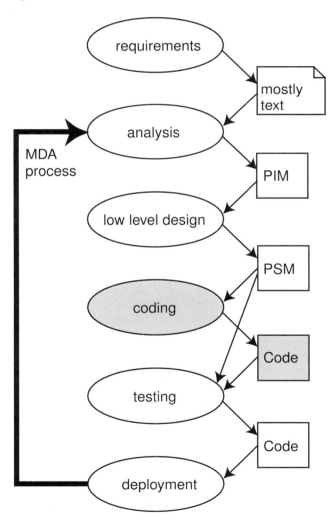

Figure 12-1 *MDA software development lifecycle revised*

In the early 1960s our industry was in the middle of a revolution. The use of existing assembly languages was substituted by the use of procedural languages. In those days, too, there was a lot of skepticism, and not without reason. The first compilers were not very good. The Algol programming language, for instance, offered a possibility to give hints to the compiler on how to translate a piece of code. Many programmers were concerned that the generated assembler code would be far less efficient than handwriting the assembler code themselves. Many could not believe that compilers would become so good that they could stop worrying about this.

To a certain extent, the skeptics were right. You lost efficiency and speed, and you couldn't program all the assembler tricks in a procedural language. However, the advantages of procedural languages became more and more obvious. Using higher level languages you can write more complex software much faster, and the resulting code is much easier to maintain. At the same time, better compiler technology diminished the disadvantages. The generated assembler code became more efficient. Today we accept the fact that we shouldn't program our systems in assembler. It is even the opposite, if someone says he is planning to write his new customer relationship management system in assembler, he would be declared insane.

What MDA brings us is a similar revolution. Eventually, PIMs can be *compiled* (read: transformed) into PSMs, which are *compiled* into procedural language code (which itself is compiled into assembly or raw machine code). The PIM to PSM *compilers* (read: transformation tools) will not be very efficient for some years to come. Its users will need to give hints on how to transform parts of a model. But eventually, the advantage of working on a higher level of abstraction will become clear to everyone in the business.

In conclusion, we can say that although the MDA is still in its infancy, it already shows the potential of changing software development radically. No, we will not tell you that from this day on you and your team will not have to write a single line of code. Of course you will need to bother with code for the next few years. Instead, we argue that you are witnessing the birth of a paradigm shift, and that in the near future software development will shift its focus from code to models.

The shift of focus from code to models will have consequences on the software development process, the languages used to write models, and the software development tools. We will examine the consequences for each in the following sections.

12.2 THE DEVELOPMENT PROCESS

What are the consequences of applying the MDA on the software development process? Comparing the MDA process to the traditional process, much will remain the same. Requirements still need to be captured and systems still need to be tested and deployed. What will change are the activities of analysis, low-level design, and coding.

During analysis a PIM will need to be developed. There will probably be a special group of people who will perform this task. They will be aware of the functionality that needs to be implemented, and they will be driven by the needs of the business and by the business model.

Most likely there will be a different group of people responsible for the transformation of the PIM to one or more PSMs. They will have knowledge of different platforms, different system architectures, and of the transformation definitions that are available for the transformation tools they are using. They will decide with what parameter values the transformations are to be applied. They will choose between various target platforms and target system architectures. Does the system require a three-layer architecture, or is a simple fat client-server architecture sufficient? Do we use J2EE or the .net as target platform? These are the kind of questions the PSM creator will need to answer. It is the responsibility of the PSM creator to be aware of and act upon quality of service aspects.

To find the answer to these questions, the PSM creator will need some information from the PIM analyst other than the PIM itself. He will need to know about the non-functional business requirements. For instance, when a PIM analyst tells the PSM creator that the system will be used intensively by over five thousand persons, the PSM creator will wisely choose another target architecture, and use another transformation definition than if the system were to be used by a group of five.

Another task of the PSM creator is to respond to changes in both the PIM and the transformation definitions. The PIM and the transformation definitions may change independently of each other. When the business requirements change, only the PIM will be affected. When the target platform changes, for instance because a new version is installed, only the transformation definition will have to be renewed. The PSM creator must respond to these changes because any change must be reflected in the generated PSM. Meanwhile, the previous version of the system that has already been deployed, may contain lots of data that has to migrate to the new version of the system. In the future this task of the PSM creator will need to be supported by tools. These tools may or may not be integrated in the transformation tool.

Because the PSM creator will need transformation definitions, buying or writing transformation definitions will be a task new to the MDA development process. In our view, there will be a third group of people who will write transformation definitions. They will partly be employed by the companies that build software systems, but a large part of this group will be employed by transformation tool vendors. Their tools will only have customer value when transformation definitions are available. Figure 12-2 shows the different participants in the MDA process, the tools they are using, and the artifacts they are producing.

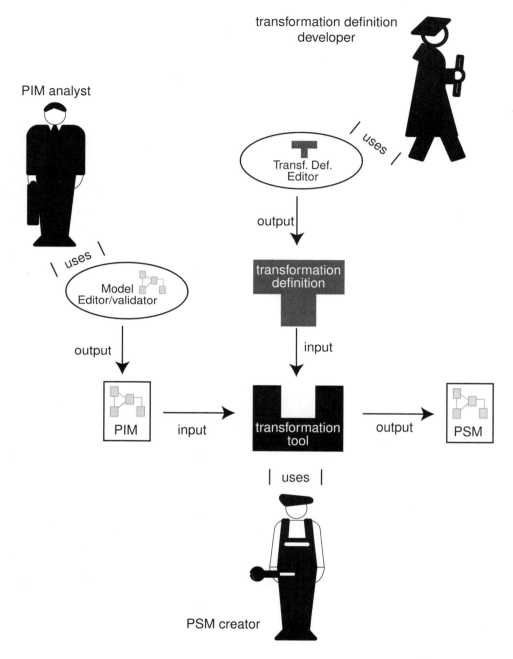

Figure 12-2 *Participants, tools, and artifacts in the MDA process*

12.3 THE TOOLS

What are the consequences of applying the MDA on the software development tools? Again, looking at the difference between the traditional development process and the MDA development process, we find three groups of people who will need new or better tools, and one group who will not need any tools, because it will not be involved in the MDA process.

The last group is the group of code writers. When the MDA approach has matured, this group will not be needed anymore. Current code writing tools, like IDEs specific to a certain programming language, will cease to be relevant in the development process. The trend is already noticeable. Currently, many IDE vendors are progressing their environments to integrate a modeling tool as well. Figure 12-3 shows how in the future the functionality supporting activities concerning code will be less important. Instead, new functionality will be demanded on the high end of the software factory pipeline.

A new kind of IDE will be demanded by the transformation definition developers. They will need specialized environments to create, edit, and test their transformation definitions. Because the aim is to reuse transformation definitions, the group of transformation definition developers will not be very large. Therefore, it is likely that there will not be a large choice of transformation definition IDEs.

The group of PSM creators will work with transformation tools. The desired functionality for these tools will include the following:

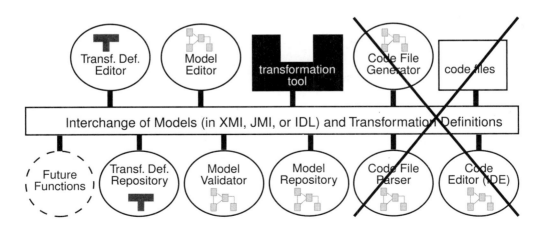

Figure 12-3 *Functionality in a future MDA development environment*

- The ability to choose between different implementation platforms
- The flexibility to switch within one platform between different implementation strategies, application architectures, and coding patterns
- Openness to plug-in multiple modeling languages, transformation definitions
- Support for standard domain specific models or blue prints
- Integration with other tools that automate software development and maintenance (code maintenance, version control, requirement management, workflow automation, testing tools, performance tuning tools, and so on)

Most likely the different tools used in the MDA process will need to interoperate or perhaps even integrate. For instance, a PSM creator may want to make a small change in the transformation definition he is using in order to produce a more efficient system. Another example is a transformation definition developer who needs to test his definition. How will he do that? The obvious choice is to use a transformation tool. Therefore, it is important that all tools operate in a standard way. Looking back at Figure 3-1 from Chapter 3, we can say that these tools must at least be able to use the same standard interchange format for models and transformation definitions.

The PIM analysts are the group that is served already. There is a large number of modeling tools available, most of which are able to read and write the standard interchange format for UML models. Still, the PIM analysts will need better modeling tools; tools that provide more support on checking the model and on the integration of the model parts. For example, the flow of information between the various UML diagrams should be supported. But most of all the PIM analyst needs better modeling languages.

12.4 THE MODELING LANGUAGES

What are the consequences of applying the MDA on the modeling languages? To be able to write PIMs that completely specify the system to be generated, including both static and dynamic aspects, we need a different set of modeling languages.

Today's modeling languages provide us with the means to specify the structural part of the functionality in a PIM. For the dynamic part, they depend on ordinary programming languages to fill in the gaps in the model. The action language used in Executable UML (Mellor and Balcer 2002) tries to fill this gap, but as explained in section 3.2.2, the available concepts are at the same abstraction level as the current procedural and object oriented languages. Unless the action language gets to a higher level of abstraction, it will not be able to support the MDA process fully.

A modeling language suited for MDA should offer the following:

- Expressive enough to specify systems completely. This includes both static and dynamic aspects of a system. There should be no need for the developers to fall back to ordinary programming languages.

- A general applicable, non application-specific, language. Application specific languages like 4GLs never really set off. Most programming is still done using generally applicable programming languages.

- Abstract often-used patterns of lower-level constructs into single higher-level constructs.

- Suitable for n-tier application development, including three-tier, two-tier, and single-tier applications. The actual number of tiers should be of no consequence in the model, but should be adjusted in the settings of the transformation tool.

- Suitable for distributed applications. Transformation tools should take care of building the bridges between the various nodes.

- Seamlessness between the model and its implementation.

- Support for managing large models, for instance by supporting an aspect-oriented manner of modeling (Kiczales 1997).

Note that when a modeling language is created that allows full specification of a system, including both static and dynamic aspects, it becomes more than a modeling language. In fact, the modeling languages of tomorrow will have the same status as the high-level programming languages of today.

12.5 SUMMARY

In this chapter we have taken a look into the crystal ball and predicted what the future of software development might look like when the MDA is applied on a large scale.

Although the MDA is still in its infancy, it already shows the potential of changing software development radically. Nowadays the focus of the software development process is on writing code. In the future the focus will shift to writing the PSM, and from there to writing the PIM. People will forget the fact that the PSM needs to be transformed into code, because generating the code will be automated. This is such a major change in the development process that it can be called a paradigm shift.

The shift of focus from code to models will have consequences on the software development process, the languages used to write models, and the software development tools. In the software development process, three participants can be recognized:

- The PSM creator, who is responsible for transforming a PIM to one or more PSMs.The PSM creator will be the one that uses transformation tools. He will choose the right transformation for the job and parameterize it.

- The transformation definition developer, who is responsible for creating and maintaining transformation definitions. The transformation definition developer will need a specialized environment to create, edit, and test his transformation definitions.

- The PIM analyst, who is responsible for creating and maintaining PIMs. The PIM analyst will need better modeling tools. But most of all the PIM analyst needs better modeling languages.

New modeling languages suited for MDA will be defined. They will allow full specification of a system, including both static and dynamic aspects. Such a language will have the same status as the programming languages of today.

Glossary

Abstraction

A broad and general term indicating (1) a less detailed model that conforms to (defines a subset of the properties of) another model, and (2) the process through which a less detailed but conforming model is made, that is, the process of removing details that are not relevant to the purpose of the model.

Abstraction Level

The inverse of the (relative) amount of details that are in a model. See *High-* and *Low Abstraction Level*.

Communication Bridge

An implementation or model of communication between two parts of a system. Mostly used in a context where the parts of the system are realized using different technologies.

Coarse Grained Component

Components that have infrequent interaction with a relatively high amount of data in each interaction.

Diagram

A visible graphical rendering of (a part of) a model.

Fine Grained Component

Components that have frequent communication with a low amount of data in each interaction.

High Abstraction Level

A (relatively) low amount of details.

Language

In this book we use the word language as a synonym for *Well-Defined Language*.

Low Abstraction Level

A (relatively) high amount of details.

Mapping

The constraining relationship between the structure of the source and target language in a transformation definition.

Mapping Rule

Synonym for *Transformation Rule*.

Metalanguage

The language used to define languages.

Metamodel

A description or definition of a well-defined language in the form of a model.

Model

A description of (part of) a system written in a well-defined language. Equivalent to Specification.

Model Driven Software Development

The process of developing software using different models on different levels of abstraction with (automated) transformations between these models.

Model Generation

A process that creates a model from another model according to some transformation rules.

Platform

A specific software implementation technology and/or specific hardware that constitutes the execution environment of a system.

Platform Independent Model (PIM)

A model that contains no details that have meaning only within a specific platform.

Platform Specific Model (PSM)

A model that contains details that have meaning only within a specific platform.

Semantics

The meaning of a model that is well-formed according to the syntax of a language.

Source Language

The Language that is the input of a transformation definition.

Source Model

The model that is the input of a transformation.

Syntax

A set of rules that define which models are well-formed in a specific language.

System

A part of the world that is the subject of a model, communication, or reasoning. In the context of this book the word system is most commonly used for a software system.

Target Language

The language that is the result of a transformation definition.

Target Model

The model that is the result of a transformation.

Transformation

The automatic generation of a target model from a source model, according to a transformation definition. Equivalent to *Mapping*.

Transformation Definition

A set of transformation rules that together describe how a model in the source language can be transformed into a model in the target language.

Transformation Definition Language

The language in which the transformation definitions are written.

Transformation Parameter

Part of a transformation definition that enables the tuning of a transformation. Transformation parameters typically add information that cannot be found in the source model but is necessary to produce the target model.

Transformation Rule

A description of how one or more constructs in the source language can be transformed into one or more constructs in the target language.

Transformation Tool

A (software) tool that is able to execute a transformation definition.

Well-Defined Language

A language with well-defined form (syntax) and meaning (semantics), which is suitable for automated interpretation by a computer.

The Code for Rosa's System

B.1 The SQL Code for Rosa's System

The following code snippet is the SQL script to create the tables for Rosa's Breakfast
Service:

```
CREATE TABLE Comestible (
    comestibleID                INTEGER                 NOT
NULL,
    name                        VARCHAR (40)            NULL,
    price                       REAL                    NULL,
    minimalQuantity             INTEGER                 NULL,
    transportForm               VARCHAR (40)            NULL,
    PRIMARY KEY (comestibleID)
);

CREATE TABLE StandardBreakfast (
    standardBreakfastID         INTEGER                 NOT
NULL,
    name                        VARCHAR (40)            NULL,
    price                       REAL                    NULL,
    style                       INTEGER                 NULL,
    PRIMARY KEY (tabelID)
);

CREATE TABLE Part (
    standardBreakfastID         INTEGER                 NOT
NULL,
    comestibleID                INTEGER                 NOT
NULL,
    quantity                    INTEGER                 NULL,
    PRIMARY KEY (standardBreakfastID, comestibleID)
);

CREATE TABLE Customer (
    customerID                  INTEGER                 NOT
```

```sql
NULL,
    accountNumber               DECIMAL                    NULL,
    addressStreet               VARCHAR (40)               NULL,
    addressCity                 VARCHAR (40)               NULL,
    addressStreetNumber         VARCHAR (40)               NULL,
    addressPostalCode           VARCHAR (40)               NULL,
    addressTelephoneNumber      VARCHAR (40)               NULL,
    PRIMARY KEY (customerID)
);

CREATE TABLE BreakfastOrder (
    breakfastOrderID            INTEGER                     NOT
NULL,
    customerId                  INTEGER                     NOT
NULL,
    orderDate                   DATE                       NULL,
    deliveryAddressStreet       VARCHAR (40)               NULL,
    deliveryAddressCity         VARCHAR (40)               NULL,
    deliveryAddressStreetNumber VARCHAR (40)               NULL,
    deliveryAddressPostalCode   VARCHAR (40)               NULL,
    deliveryAddressTelephoneNumber VARCHAR (40)
NULL,
    deliveryDate                DATE                       NULL,
    deliveryTime                TIME                       NULL,
    discount                    REAL                       NULL,
    PRIMARY KEY (breakfastOrderID)
);

CREATE TABLE Breakfast (
    breakfastID                 INTEGER                     NOT
NULL,
    breakfastOrderID            INTEGER                     NOT
NULL,
    standardBreakfastID         INTEGER                     NOT
NULL,
    number                      INTEGER                    NULL,
    PRIMARY KEY (breakfastID)
);

CREATE TABLE Change (
    breakfastID                 INTEGER                     NOT
NULL,
    comestibleID                INTEGER                     NOT
NULL,
    quantity                    INTEGER                    NULL,
    PRIMARY KEY (breakfastId, comestibleID)
);
```

B.2 The EJB Code for Rosa's System

The following code sniplet describes the remote interface of the entity bean called *BreakfastOrder:*

```
import java.rmi.*;
import javax.naming.*;
import javax.ejb.*;
import breakfast.ejb.breakfastorder.*;

public interface BreakfastOrder extends EJBObject {

    public BreakfastOrderDataObject getBreakfastOrder()
                    throws  RemoteException;

    public void setBreakfastOrder(BreakfastOrderDataObject update)
                    throws  NamingException,
                            FinderException,
                            CreateException,
                            RemoteException;

    public float calculatePrice()
                    throws RemoteException;
}
```

The following code snippet shows the implementation of the data class for *BreakfastOrder*:

```
import breakfast.ejb.*;
import java.util.*;

public class BreakfastOrderDataObject
                        extends DataObject implements
java.io.Serializable {

    private BreakfastOrderKey key;

    /**
     * Creates a new BreakfastOrderDataObject.
     * @param key initialize all fields necessary to uniquely
identify
     * this object
     */
    public BreakfastOrderDataObject(BreakfastOrderKey key) {
        this.key = key;
        this.deliveryAddress = new Address();
    }

    public int getBreakfastOrderID() {
```

```
            return key.getBreakfastOrderID();
    }

    // References to associated single classes:
    private CustomerKey customercustomerKey;

    /**
     * Sets the foreign key CustomerKey of the singular referenced
     * Customer
     * @param  CustomerKey
     */
    public void setCustomerCustomer(CustomerKey s) {
        this.customercustomerKey = s;
    }

    /**
     * Returns the foreign key CustomerKey of the singular
referenced Customer
     * @return  CustomerKey
     */
    public CustomerKey getCustomerCustomer() {
        return customercustomerKey;
    }

    // References to by-value-treated collections of objects:

    private
breakfast.ejb.breakfastorder.BreakfastDataObjectCollection
                            breakfastbreakfast;

    public void addBreakfast(
            breakfast.ejb.breakfastorder.BreakfastDataObject added)
{
        this.breakfastbreakfast.add(added);
    }

    public void removeBreakfast(
            breakfast.ejb.breakfastorder.BreakfastDataObject
removed) {
        this.breakfastbreakfast.remove(removed);
    }

    /**
     * Returns the internal BreakfastDataObjectCollection of the
multiple
     * contained Breakfast.
     * @return breakfast.ejb.breakfastorder.
     *                              BreakfastDataObjectCollection
```

```
        */
    public
breakfast.ejb.breakfastorder.BreakfastDataObjectCollection
            getBreakfast() {
        if (breakfast == null) {
            breakfast =
        new
breakfast.ejb.breakfastorder.BreakfastDataObjectListImpl();
        }
        return breakfast;
    }

    // No associated collections of objects by reference

    // Attributes:

    private java.util.Date orderDate;

    /**
     * Returns attribute orderDate.
     * @return java.util.Date
     */
    public java.util.Date getOrderDate() {
      return  orderDate;
    }

    public void setOrderDate(java.util.Date value) {
        this.orderDate = value;
    }

    private Address deliveryAddress;

    /**
     * Returns a copy of attribute deliveryAddress.
     * Since deliveryAddress is a StructType, we do not want that the
     * object returned by getDeliveryAddress() can implicitly change
the
     * state of the owner BreakfastOrder.
     * Therefore a copy is returned.
     * @return Address
     */
    public Address getDeliveryAddress() {
      return deliveryAddress != null ? deliveryAddress.deepCopy() :
null;
    }

    public void setDeliveryAddress(Address value) {
        this.deliveryAddress = value;
```

```java
      }

   private java.util.Date deliveryDate;

   /**
    * Returns attribute deliveryDate.
    * @return java.util.Date
    */
   public java.util.Date getDeliveryDate() {
     return  deliveryDate;
   }

   public void setDeliveryDate(java.util.Date value) {
       this.deliveryDate = value;
   }

   private java.util.Date deliveryTime;

   /**
    * Returns attribute deliveryTime.
    * @return java.util.Date
    */
   public java.util.Date getDeliveryTime() {
     return  deliveryTime;
   }

   public void setDeliveryTime(java.util.Date value) {
       this.deliveryTime = value;
   }

   private floatdiscount;

   /**
    * Returns attribute discount.
    * @return float
    */
   public float getDiscount() {
     return  discount;
   }

   public void setDiscount(float value) {
       this.discount = value;
   }

}
```

B.3 The JSP Code for Rosa's System

```
<%-- Page Directives  --%>
<%@ page import    = "java.util.*" %>
<%@ page import    = "breakfast.ejb.*"%>
<%@ page import    = "breakfast.ejb.customer.*"%>
<%@ page errorPage ="AppError.jsp" %>
<%-- Include Directives --%>

<%-- Tag Library Directives --%>

<%-- Variable and Method declarations --%>
<%!
Collection CustomerCollection;
CustomerDataObject Customer;
Iterator it;
%>
<%-- Actions --%>
<jsp:useBean id="CustomerDom" scope="request"
class="breakfast.ejb.CustomerDataObjectManager"/>

<HTML>
<head>
<title>moduleseparatorCustomer</title>
<link href="css/ApplicationStyle.css" rel="stylesheet" type="text/
css" />
</head>
<body>
<table class="layout-table">

<tr class="layout-row"><td class="layout-cell">


<p>
This Page illustrates how a Retrieve is executed on the EJB tier.
</p>
<p>
It is written as pure Jsp, with a connection to basic OptimalJ
data-structures.
</p>
<p></p>
<table align="center" border="1" summary="">
  <!-- table heading -->
  <tr>
    <th align=left><font size="5"><b>Customer</b></font></th>
  </tr>
  <tr>
    <td align=left><font size="3"><b>id</b></font></td>
```

```
      <td align=left><font size="3"><b>address</b></font></td>
      <td align=left><font size="3"><b>accountNumber</b></font></td>
   </tr>
   <!-- table data -->
   <%
   // let Remote View Manager retrieve data
   CustomerCollection = CustomerDom.retrieve();

   it = CustomerCollection.iterator();

   // iterate collection and write data elements
   while (it.hasNext()) {
     Customer = (CustomerDataObject) it.next();
     request.setAttribute("Customer", Customer);
   %>
   <tr>
      <td align=left><font size="3"><jsp:getProperty name="Customer"
property="id"/></font></td>
      <td align=left><font size="3"><jsp:getProperty name="Customer"
property="address"/></font></td>
      <td align=left><font size="3"><jsp:getProperty name="Customer"
property="accountNumber"/></font></td>
   </tr>
   <%
   }
   %>
</table>
<p></p>
</td></tr>

</table>

</body>

</HTML>
```

Bibliography

Allen, Paul, and Stuart Frost. *Component-Based Development for Enterprise Systems.* Cambridge, U.K.: Cambridge University Press, 1998.

Beck, Kent. *Extreme Programming Explained: Embrace Change.* Boston: Addison-Wesley, 2000.

Blaha, Michael, and William Premerlani. *Object-Oriented Modeling and Design for Database Applications.* Upper Saddle River, NJ.: Prentice Hall, 1998.

Booch, Grady, James Rumbaugh, and Ivar Jacobson. *The Unified Modeling Language User Guide.* Reading, MA.: Addison-Wesley, 1999.

Carnegie Mellon University/Software Engineering Institute. *The Capability Maturity Model, Guidelines for Improving the Software Process.* Boston: Addison-Wesley, 1995.

Cheesman, John, and John Daniels. *UML Components, A Simple Process for Specifying Component-Based Software.* Boston: Addison-Wesley, 2001.

Cockburn, Alistair. *Agile Software Development.* Boston: Addison-Wesley, 2002.

Frankel, David. *Model Driven Architecture: Applying MDA to Enterprise Computing.* New York: John Wiley & Sons, 2003.

Hubert, Richard. *Convergent Architecture: Building Model-Driven J2EE Systems with UML.* New York: John Wiley & Sons, 2001.

ISO/IEC. *Information Technology—Database Languages—SQL.* Washington DC: ISO/IEC 9075:1992.

Java Community. *UML/EJB Mapping Specification.* Process document JSR26, 2001.

Kennedy Carter. *Supporting Model Driven Architecture with eXecutable UML.* White Paper CTN 80, v2.2.

Kiczales, Gregor, et al. *Aspect Oriented Programming.* Proceedings, European Conference on Object-Oriented Programming.

Meyer, Bertrand. *Object-Oriented Software Construction, Second Edition.* Upper Saddle River, NJ.: Prentice-Hall, 1997.

Mellor, Stephen J., and Marc J. Balcer. *Executable UML: A Foundation for Model-Driven Architecture.* Boston: Addison Wesley, 2002.

OMG. *CWM 1.1 Specification.* formal/2001-10-01 and formal/2001-10-27.

OMG. *MOF 1.4 Specification.*formal/2002-04-03.

OMG. *Object Constraint Language 2.0 Submission.* ad/02-05-09.

OMG. *UML 1.4 Action Semantics.* ptc/2002-01-09.

OMG. *UML 1.4 Specification.* formal/2001-09-67.

Rumbaugh, James, Grady Booch and Ivar Jacobson. *Unified Modeling Language Reference Manual.* Reading, MA.: Addison-Wesley, 1999.

Selic, Bran, Garth Gullekson, and Paul T. Ward. *Real-Time Object-Oriented Modeling.* New York: John Wiley & Sons, 1994.

Sun Microsystems. *Enterprise JavaBeans Specification, Version 2.1.* JSR-153, 2002.

Sun Microsystems. *Java 2 Platform, Enterprise Edition Specification, Version 1.3.* 2002.

Sun Microsystems. *Java Metadata Interface Specification, Version 1.0.* 2002.

Sun Microsystems. *JavaServer Pages Specification, Version 1.2.* 2001.

Szyperski, Clemens, *Component Software, Beyond Object-Oriented Programming.* Harlow, U.K.: Addison-Wesley, 1998.

Warmer, Jos, and Anneke Kleppe. *The Object Constraint Language, Precise Modeling with UML.* Reading, MA.: Addison-Wesley, 1999.

Warmer, Jos, and Anneke Kleppe. *The Object Constraint Language, Getting Your Models Ready for MDA.* Forthcoming.

Index

Symbols
<~> 97

A
abstraction level 8, 11, 36, 37, 41, 47, 65,
    78, 150
Action Semantics
    See AS
Agile Software Development 2, 40
analysis 2, 147
AS 33, 35, 138
assembler languages 144
association 29, 101
    multiplicity 29
attribute 101

B
Backus Naur Form
    See BNF
bidirectionality 77, 97
BNF 83
business
    metadata 139
    method 120
    model 19
    rules 36

C
CASE tool 37, 39
CIM 19
coarse grained component model 55, 113
code 6
    bridge 10
    generation 37

model 63
coding 2
Common Warehouse Metamodel
    See CWM
composite aggregation 55, 116, 124
Computational Independent Model
    See CIM
conceptualization 2
constraint 140
container managed persistency 65
controlling transformations 74
CORBA
    IDL 132
    Profile 34, 140
CWM 34, 87, 131, 138, 139

D
data mining 139
data object manager 67
deployment 2
    descriptor 65
design 2
    decision 30
documentation 5, 11
dynamic model 20
dynamic view 20

E
EAI 34
    Profile 34
EDOC 34
    Profile 34
EJB 4, 45, 114
    container 65

Register
Your Book

at www.awprofessional.com/register

You may be eligible to receive:

- Advance notice of forthcoming editions of the book
- Related book recommendations
- Chapter excerpts and supplements of forthcoming titles
- Information about special contests and promotions throughout the year
- Notices and reminders about author appearances, tradeshows, and online chats with special guests

Contact us

If you are interested in writing a book or reviewing manuscripts prior to publication, please write to us at:

Editorial Department
Addison-Wesley Professional
75 Arlington Street, Suite 300
Boston, MA 02116 USA
Email: AWPro@aw.com

Visit us on the Web: http://www.awprofessional.com